A

MISCELLANY

OF

INFORMATION

Magical and Otherwise

By
Draja Mickaharic

Lulu, Inc.
Morrisville, NC
USA

First Published in 2010 by
Lulu, Inc.
860 Aviation Parkway   Suite 300
Morrisville, NC   27560

Lulu Enterprises, Inc.
3101 Hillsborough Street
Raleigh, NC   27607

www.Lulu.com

Voice: 919-459-5858

Fax: 919-459-5867

ISBN 978-1-257-64471-1
LCCN

Printed in the United States of America

PREFACE

Over the years I have printed up what might be called handouts for both my students and my clients. Many of the handouts I gave my clients were published in my "Spiritual Workers Spell Book." Most of the handouts I gave my students are located in this book. Thus this book is a miscellany concerning a variety of subjects, although it is less philosophical than my book, A Magical Pie.

One of the items that may be of general interest is a set of spells I have used to encourage the economic evolution of my students. Everyone has periods in which their income is not sufficient to support them. This is the reason savings are urged on people. However, I have found people usually do not pay themselves first by saving a part of their income every payday. When money is required, I have used these spells to assist my students in increasing their income, or obtaining gainful employment.

There are also a few other spells I have found useful, but in the main this book consists of things I wished my students to either practice or learn as a part of their being. Gathering all these papers up has been a chore, as most of them were either misfiled or placed in boxes I had sent to storage. However, here they are, and I hope you find them both interesting and useful.

With my sincere best wishes for your continued success,
Draja Mickaharic

THE PURPOSE OF MAGIC

The purpose of magic is not to produce amazement and wonder, but to produce certain functional effects -- much as the purpose of a flashlight is to produce light when it its turned on, - and not otherwise.

The fact that some people like to participate in so called magical rituals is very similar to the fact that some people like to eat candy. Enjoying something does not mean that you are gaining any real benefit from it.

CONTENTS

1

GYPSY CARD READING

The information below may explain why I don't believe in consulting storefront Readers and Advisors. The following is taken from the information one of these "Gypsy Card Readers," gave me when she consulted me about a personal problem.

"This is the 'Gypsy Street Method' of reading ordinary playing cards. It is done with a standard poker deck of playing cards, without any jokers. It assumes that you have memorized several lines of 'patter,' of the kind used in 'Gypsy Cold Readings.' This 'patter' is used to fill in the spaces in your reading. When you give a reading you should always speak confidently, as if you were certain of what you said, and definitely speak your words as a past, present or future event in the life of the person. The delivery of your reading, and the way you read for your client, is at least as important as what you tell the client.

Always discuss positive character traits as being in the present. Do not discuss negative character traits at all.

(1)   Have the client separate the cards into three ap-proximately equal piles.   There should be approximately seventeen cards in each pile. (52/3 = 17 1/3)

(2)   Have the client select one of these three piles. Pick up and quickly put away the other two piles. Get them out of sight immediately.

(3)   Have the client take four (or five – your choice) cards from the remaining pile.

(4)   Turn them face up in front of the client, in the space between you and her.

(5)   Begin giving the reading, based on the following guidelines:

Card Meanings

<u>King of Hearts</u> – The Male client, the primary male figure, or the lover when reading for a female client.

<u>Queen of Hearts</u> – The female client or the primary female figure, or the lover when reading for a male client.

<u>Ace of Spades</u> – Death or serious injury, depending on the supporting cards. When you are reading this as death, you must note which cards are next to the ace of spades to determine whom this death pertains to. If it is the King of Hearts when reading for a male client, or the Queen of Hearts when reading for a female client, it is the client's death. If the death of a client is clearly shown, it is best to want the client only of 'There is a strong potential for you to be involved in an accident,' and urge them to take great caution in their affairs.

<u>Seven of any Suite</u> - Relates to the client's home.

<u>Eight of any Suite</u> - Relates to correspondence or com-munication of some kind, (including Emails.)

<u>Nine of any Suite</u> - Relates to thought, ideas, verbal communication, or education.

<u>Ten of any Suite</u> - Relates to Travel, a change of scene, and possibly a change of work.

The Suites Of The Cards Determine Their Value
Or Their Impact In The Life of The Client.

The red suites are favorable to the client
Diamonds relate to money
Hearts relate to Love

The black suites are unfavorable for the client

Clubs relate to trouble – Spades relate to serious injury, illness or, as with the ace of spades, death. Spades always require that a warning of some kind be given to the client.

Face cards deal with relationships of the client to others. The suite of the face card and the numeric value of the surrounding cards determine the relationship and it's impact on the client.

Odd numbered cards deal with men, while Even numbered cards deal with women.

As an example, in this reading: A three of clubs next to a ten of diamonds indicates that, the reader "sees there will be a trip involving money, but there will be some trouble involved in either the trip or in gaining the money." With a two of clubs, there is an indication of a little trouble, while the ace of clubs indicates a great deal of trouble. You must read the cards as they are, surrounding each other.

MISCELLANY

Learn to read the cards as if you were reading a book, following the above guidelines. If you are not sure what you see, go with your first instinct. The cards are really only a channel for your reading. Once you learn to master listening, you will discover the client will tell you everything you need to know. Watch the client's responses to what you tell them. Their body language will tell you as much as their words.

In time, as your intuition opens, you will receive defiant impressions about people. You should voice only those impressions you believe the client will accept as being favorable to them.

One of the most important things to know about reading for others is the following.

Most people do not want to hear about their future unless it is good.

Most people do not have a good future ahead of them.

2

LIFE EVENT BATHS FOR WOMEN

A CLEANSING BATH FOLLOWING A GIRLS FIRST MENSTRUAL PERIOD

A young girls first menstruation can be a traumatic and often unexpected experience for her. Once she is adapted to it, and her first menstruation ends, a special bath can often sooth her nerves, calm, her fears, and remove some of the shock and surprise her initial menstruation caused her.

Because pink, yellow, and light blue colors all relate to femininity, the clothing to be worn after the bath should be one of these colors. The bath itself should be reasonably warm, but not hot. As it is a spiritual bath, the girl should remain in it five to eight minutes and completely immerse herself five times.

An excellent bath for this purpose can be made from:
    Five yellow roses
    A teaspoon of honey
    And a pinch of salt

These materials are added to the bath, and the water in the tub stirred. The girl then enters the tub and immerses herself. She may then scrub her face and head with one of the yellow roses, and immerse herself again. She should then scrub her sex with another rose, and immerse a third time. Pouring water over her head and immersing two more times completes the bath.

As with any spiritual bath, the girl should air dry, and then dress in clean clothing of one of the colors mentioned above.

NOTE: I strongly endorse the idea of fully explaining the process of menstruation to young girls when they are six or seven, and continuing the explanation every year until they begin menstruating. Doing this will minimize the shock of their first menstrual period. I am aware this is not very often done, but I do believe it is a good idea.

A BRIDAL RITUAL AND BATH

In Zora Neale Hurston's book, "Tell My Horse," she describes a ritual that was performed for a bride in preparation for her wedding. Zora Neale Hurston witnessed both the ritual and the wedding in Jamaica.

On the wedding day, an old woman instructs the bride to be in how to have sex in a good way. She then gives the young woman a 'balm bath,' which is a hot bath made with herbs that were unknown to Ms. Hurston. The old woman who was bathing her told the bride to be that, "This bath is to remove everything physical, mental, and spiritual, that might work against your having a happy mating."

After her bath the girl is covered to sweat for a while. Later she is bathed in soapy water. The older woman then massages the bride's body all over with vetiver oil, arouses her with touch, and tickles her with a feather. She then receives a sip of rum in which a single leaf of Ganga (Marijuana) has been steeped. The bride is then eager to meet her husband to be.

BATHS FOR WOMEN

Ganga is said to be the "Wisdom weed," that was thought to have been brought to Jamaica from the river Ganges in India. In fact, the herb was probably native to Jamaica.

There is a similar bridal bath given on page 202 of "Hoodoo Herb and Root Magic," By Cat Yronwode. One of the similarities between them is the use of Vetiver.

I believe a pre-marital bath, similar to that described, and counsel from an experienced woman is beneficial for any woman either before her first sexual experience or her wedding. I am well aware that today the first sexual experience usually occurs long before the wedding. However, such a bath and receiving honest intimate counsel from the girl's mother or an aunt would prove to be of benefit to her.

I also believe that it would be beneficial for a family to develop a regular set of private rituals for these life events. Menstruation, Copulation, and Marriage are all life changing events, especially for a woman, and if the family recognizes them with rituals, it would seem to make it easier to hold the family together.

BLACKHAWK IN A BUCKET
AN INTRODUCTION TO WORKING WITH SPIRITUAL FORCES

The spirit of Blackhawk (1767 – 1838), the Illinois born In-
dian Chief of the Sauk and Fox tribes, who was an ally of the
British in the war of 1812, and led a consortium of Native
American tribes in the Blackhawk war, is one of the major spirits worked with by members of some of the Spiritualist
Churches today. The Blackhawk war (1831-1832), which offi-
cially began April 14th, 1832, was fought along the Mississippi
river, encompassing parts of the area now occupied by Missouri,
Iowa, Illinois, and Wisconsin. Primarily fought in Illinois and
Wisconsin, the Blackhawk war ended with the defeat of the In-
dian tribes at the battle of Bad Axe River in Wisconsin. The
Blackhawk war is neither particularly well known, nor well re-
membered today.

One of the long-term results of the Blackhawk war was a tall
statue of Blackhawk erected along the Rock River at Oregon
Illinois. Abraham Lincoln, initially as a member of the 31st
regiment of the Illinois Militia, was involved in the Blackhawk
war from April 21st to July 11th, 1832. Serving first as the
elected captain of his company and later as a private soldier, he
saw no combat service. Nonetheless he was probably the most

notable combatant of that war, which involved many future governors and other future public officials as members and officers of both the militia and the regular army units involved.

The former 87th infantry division, sometimes a reserve airborne division, is said to have descended from the infantry company of the 31st Illinois Abraham Lincoln led in the Blackhawk war. This division is known as the 'rail splitters,' in his memory.

~~~~~~~~~~~

I know of no reason why the spirit of Blackhawk became so popular in the Spiritual Church community. The many Indian spirits who abounded during the heyday of the spiritualist movement in the late 1800's and early 1900's were certainly not limited to those associated with Blackhawk. There were hundreds of these Indian 'spirit guides,' most with exotic names ranging from Dawn Flower to Chief Iroquois. How Blackhawk gained the lead, and became a permanent spirit associated with spiritual workers and the Spiritualist Church movement, is unknown to me.

When the symbol of Blackhawk is found in the workrooms or altars of spiritual workers or in Spiritualist Churches today, it is usually manifested as his plaster statue placed in a galvanized bucket. This placement of Blackhawk's statue in a bucket is thought to have been adopted from the naganga or cauldron of the African Kongo Palo religion, and similar African spirit working practices. As in the Palo practice, offerings are given to the statue in his bucket.

Many individual spiritual workers work with the spirit of Blackhawk. Some of the instructions for working with the spirit of Blackhawk are given below. Much of the following material comes from Marc Richard, a.k.a. Dr. Love Bug. Other information comes from Star Casas, as well as Cat Yronwode and a few other Spiritualist and Hoodoo spiritual workers.

The most important part of working with Blackhawk is your ability to call him. This is true of working with any spiritual force. If you can call the spirit, and the spirit responds to you, it means you can work with that spirit, and the spirit will work with you. If the spirit does not respond to you, if it does not answer your call, you will not be able to successfully work with that spirit.

One of the best signs you are intended to work with a specific spirit is that you are drawn to that spirit, or you find you have a desire to work with it. You may find that you are running into pictures or statues of that spirit, or seeing some of the signs of that spirit around you. One woman who was intended to work with Blackhawk found she began seeing black hawks around her home. Soon she noticed they were always around her, wherever she went. Then a family of black hawks moved into a tree in her front yard. She soon began successfully working with the spirit of Blackhawk, and has done so for several years.

TO WORK WITH A SPIRITUAL FORCE

This applies to working with a spiritual force, like the Spirit of Blackhawk, not working with the human dead. For example, you could work with Calistro or the Cornelius Agrippa in this way, but only as a spiritual force. These formerly incarnate beings, like Blackhawk, have attracted a number of people who have, by their emotional admiration for them, built a spiritual force around these beings. It is the spiritual force you are working with, not the spirit of the deceased individual.

To learn if you can get the sprit of Blackhawk, or any other spirit to respond to you, place the statue, or a picture, of the spirit in front of you and stare into the eyes. Meditate on the spirit for a few minutes while continuing to stare into the eyes of the statue. Call on the spirit, asking it to work with you. Say aloud something like:

> Blackhawk I call on you to talk to me and
> work with me in the name of spirit. In the name
> of Jesus I ask you to come to me and work with
> me. Give Voice to me, and Give Me Power.

In this prayer, especially in the last part, you are calling on the spirit you are addressing to speak to you, so the spirit can instruct you. Now sprinkle fresh water on the statue of the spirit in a clockwise motion to 'wake it up.' You will know the spirit is there with you, as you will feel its power when you begin this rite. Now pour a shot glass of whiskey on the statue, or offer it to the picture. This washes him, cleans him, and prepares the statue to receive the spirit.

> Note: Some people use sugar water, or honey water instead of whisky or rum. They do this either because they have an aversion to whisky and rum, or because they believe Blackhawk, who was a non-drinker, has an aversion to whisky. These people seem to be able to work with Blackhawk as well as those who offer him whisky. I believe this is only a matter of personal preference and belief, although I know that offering whisky, rum, and other alcoholic beverages to spirits of the dead and spiritual forces generally is a very common practice.

Once you have washed and cleansed the statue of Blackhawk, you should present gifts to the spirit. This may be smoke, as in blowing cigar smoke on the statue, offering tobacco, giving offerings of cooked vegetables such as peas and corn, or offering the spirit feathers, or fruits. You should only offer Blackhawk foods that Native Americans ate.

If you are working with any other spiritual force, you must first research and learn the likes and dislikes of the spirit you wish to work with. This is hardly unique to Blackhawk, as it applies to all spiritual forces of the non-physical invisible universe. Check libraries, the Internet, and check with other spiritual workers to learn about these forces before you begin working with them.

You can also burn candles to Blackhawk. When burning candles to him, you should state:

'I offer this candle to the spirit of Blackhawk.'

MISCELLANY

If you are offering this candle for a specific thing, as a reward or as an inducement, you should mention the purpose of the candle in your dedication, which is to be made as you light the candle. Naturally you must always mention the spirit whom you are lighting the candle for.

You must be aware there are some spirits you should never light candles to. In many cases, these are spirits that deal with fire and conflagration, but there are other spirits who can get really annoyed if you burn a candle to them. This is one reason why you have to investigate the spirits likes and dislikes before you try and work with them.

When working with Blackhawk, and several other spirits, you will have to give them tools. Many warrior spirits will need to be given weapons, so they can protect you, and cover your back. A knife and a hatchet are good weapons for Blackhawk, as are a spear and a bow with some arrows. An iron spike, a leather medicine bag, and a few arrowheads make a good addition to the bucket in which Blackhawk is kept. When in doubt you should ask the spirit what it wants. The answer may surprise you, but whatever it is you should give it to them. Whatever the spirit wants will come to you if you pray for it.

Many people put earth or dirt in the bucket in which the statue of Blackhawk is kept. This dirt may be taken from a crossroads, a cemetery, or some other place. It is best to ask the spirit if it wishes to have dirt in the bucket, and if so, where the dirt should be obtained. As an example, if you want to do court-case work, dirt from a court, and dirt from a prison make useful additions to the bucket in which the statue of Blackhawk is kept. Graveyard dirt from a variety of graves, 'Unspecified graveyard dirt,' is often used in buckets.

Sometimes broom corn, with the seed still on the stalks are placed in the bucket. This is done to sweep away the dust of time, and to acknowledge the numerous decedents of these ancestral spirits.

If you feel the spirit wants you to put something in the bucket, you should do your best to get it for them. You need only pray for it and it will come to you.

BLACKHAWK IN A BUCKET

Once you place Blackhawk in his bucket with his tools, you should sprinkle cool water around him in a clockwise direction occasionally. Do this once a week unless you are making the spirit work hard, then you may need to sprinkle him with water more frequently, sometimes every day.

Washing the statue of the spirit in cool running water, and sprinkling the statue and his bucket with Florida water refreshes the spirit. This should be done at least annually, and is often done on June 24th, the feast day of St John the Baptist. Some Spiritual Churches use Indian spirits, and in particular Blackhawk, as stand-ins for St. John the Baptist. This is why his annual cleansing and refreshment ceremony is often conducted on June 24th.

It is advisable to talk to the spirit frequently; you should address him every day if you have a daily duty at your altar. You should greet the spirit and ask it to assist you in your everyday life. One prayer or greeting you could use is:

> Father Blackhawk, I wish your guidance in my life to help me improve the circumstances of my life, allow me to make progress, and to do well with my life. Aid me in growing, and help me be successful in my life, both financially and spiritually. Protect my friends and I, keep my enemies far away from me. Lead me to attaining God's intended potential for me. Amen

Using The Correct Statue

The best statue of Blackhawk to place in your galvanized bucket is a statue that is a bust of him. In many of these statues he wears a necklace, and often a feathered headdress. There is another statue of Blackhawk showing him holding a cow head with horns. This statue is used to protect a home, and is not meant to be placed into a bucket.

The statue of Blackhawk with the horned cow head is to be placed outside of the house, by the front door. It may be enlivened and prayed over to protect the house. It can be placed on the front porch, sheltered from the weather from where it will protect the home. It too should be sprinkled with cool water at least once each week.

Getting Help And Guidance From Blackhawk

Believed to be a particular friend of African Americans, the Indian spirit guide Blackhawk is most frequently sought after as a guardian, a protector, and a 'Watcher on the wall." He is asked for help with court cases, assistance by those going to jail, and in matters of financial improvement. Blackhawk is also seen as a shield and guide, a protector of the spiritualist against the temptations, evils, and violence, of the city streets.

In general, Indian spirits are seen as being protective, and helpful guides. It is said that Blackhawk does not do dirty work, thus he is not used for harming, killing, cursing or destroying people. His is used to seek justice in legal matter, thus he is most popular in court casework, both civil and criminal work, and in cases applying to those going to jail.

Statues of Blackhawk are often used as protective doorway spirits, similar to those of Ellegua, Ogun, Ochossi, and Legba.

Blackhawk's colors are red, black, and white. A banner of White, Black, and Red – or White, Red, and Black, may be used to symbolize his presence in a particular place, or at the doorway.

Reference: The Spirit Of Black Hawk: A Mystery Of Africans And Indians. By Jason Berry

4

DEVELOPING YOUR MEMORY

There are a number of tricks you may use as an aid to re-membering things, but they all rely on a single bit of knowl-edge, the knowledge is that your memories are held in place by your emotions. This means if you wish to memorize something, you will have to add emotion to it to have it remain available to your conscious mind. All of the very many tricks and tech-niques used to retain all kinds of information rely on this simple fact.

This is why it is easy for anyone to recall those things that they find exciting, or emotionally charged. These events all have lots of emotional energy in them. If you wish to remem-ber something, you should try and find some emotion to add to the memory.

Your ability to recall depends a great deal on applying all of your senses to the act of remembering. This is why it is easier for most people to recall songs or poems than it is for them to recall prose. Can you recall any of the songs you learned as a child? Most people can recall several of them easily. Advertis-ers know how easy it is for people to remember emotionally stimulating words, and they use jingles, songs, and rhymes in their advertising to get you to remember their products.

MISCELLANY

Can you recall the tune to this Pepsi jingle?
Pepsi cola hits the spot
Twelve full ounces that's a lot

Can you recall the rest of the jingle?

Many of us who are in our fifties, or are older can, even though we have not heard the jingle for many years.

This is just an example of how a song, rhyme, or jingle can stick with you. You can recall it even after not having thought about it for years. One of the methods you can use to remember things is to make a rhyme out of what you wish to recall. It is just one of a number of techniques useful for improving your memory.

Another of the techniques used to remember a list of things is to make an acronym of the first letters of the list. We can recall the names of the great lakes by recalling the phrase HOMES, which shows us the great lakes are Huron, Ontario, Michigan, Erie, and Superior.

Another is Roy G Bvi, which gives us the colors of the rainbow, Red Orange, Yellow, Green, Blue, Violet, and Indigo.

Please Excuse My Dear Aunt Susan reveals the sequence of mathematical operations in solving a formula, Parentheses, Exponents, Multiplication, Division, Addition, and Subtraction.

There are many other acronyms; some of them are specific to certain trades, such as the NEMA Resistor color code acronym, used in the electronics industry. Bad Boys Rob Our Young Girls But Violet Gives Willingly, the initials of the words standing for the colors that represent numbers, Black 0, Brown 1, Red 2, Orange 3, Yellow 4, Green 5, Blue 6, Violet 7, Gray 8, White 9.

Others acronyms are of more general interest, such as HOMES.

If we have to remember a list, say a shopping list, we can recall it in the same way, although for many things of this sort, it is better to develop the habit of writing down the items and tasks involved. Sharing the memory load between paper and your mind will keep you from over cluttering your mind with trivia. It is often easier to remember something than it is to forget it.

Apples, Bread, Milk, Butter, and Coffee can be summed ABBCM, or A Big BCM, however you wish to phase it.

A similar technique is the linking technique, connection similar things together with something else you can associate all of them with. This technique is also called association. It is another useful technique you may use in remembering things. For example, in the above list of groceries you might think of them as ingredients for an apple pie, to be enjoyed with a cup of coffee. Linking things is a very useful technique, as you can usually find something to link the things you wish to recall.

Association is a technique in which you may also connect things you wish to remember together, by associating them with something that possibly has more meaning to you, or with which you can make an emotional connection. For example, when someone says a word, other words associated with the first word or idea come to your mind. This is known as association, and is often used by psychologists to try and understand what a persons sub-conscious motivations are. For example, when you think of an apple, most people think of red. Thus to recall that a particular automobile was red, you might think of it as being apple red.

Recalling a persons name in this way we might link the name in our memory to some of his features. For example, Mr. Thomas Jones is a tall bald Welch man. We might recall him as, 'Tall bald Thomas Jones from Wales.'

Another useful linkage is to identify the persons name with the color of their eyes. The act of looking the person in the eye will often have a positive effect on them, as well as allowing you to take note of their eye color. Blue-eyed Mr. Jones can be expanded into: Tall bald blue eyed Mr. Jones from Wales.

In either case, we must always have a strong desire to recall the person's name, a desire to which emotion has been added. We may add some emotion to the interchange by deciding we wish to actively recall the name and features of Mr.

Jones. By making this important to us, some strong emotion is added to the interchange.

If you have a good visual memory, you can imagine yourself taking a photograph of Mr. Jones. In the event of a long interaction, you could present it to your mind as a motion picture. When your interaction with others is over, at your first opportunity, you should write out the details of your interaction with the person or people you meet. To be good at this visual technique you must see things vividly, see them in motion, and add emotion to what you see. The purpose of writing out the details later is to relieve and refresh your memory of the experienced, and to make your memories of the experience permanent. Naturally, the more emotion you place in the memory as it occurs, by vividly seeing the interchange, and actively desiring to recall it, the stronger your recall of the event will be.

Mastering the art of writing your experiences out in detail afterwards makes it possible for you to master the art of writing, as well as placing those things you write more firmly in your memory. The act of writing something will add emotion to the memory, as well as placing it more fully in your memory.

This can work to you benefit in other ways as well. If you have something complex you wish to remember, and you have an explanation or exposition of what it is you wish to recall, such as the explanation of a theory or process in a textbook, you might try copying this exposition out in long hand. The process of copying it out will assist the information in coming into your memory, and the emotional force of writing it out in long hand, something I am reasonably sure your rarely do, will usually add sufficient emotion to allow it to remain in your memory.

Developing your memory is like developing muscles. You need not have any particular goal in sight; you only need to have a real desire to improve your memory. Should you simply wish to develop your memory you might try memorizing one verse of a poem every day. The poem does not matter, so long as it has about ten or twenty verses. Your goal is that at the end of so many days as there are verses in the poem, you will be able to recite the entire poem from memory without any difficulty.

Should you obtain a small book of poetry you will be able to memorize one poem after another until, by the time you have finished memorizing them all, you will have not only memorized the book, you will also have greatly expanded your memory. This is the kind of mnemonic exercises that were given schoolboys two hundred years ago. It developed in them a powerful memory, which made it possible for them to learn a vast variety of facts, and have them all ready at their fingertips.

The great orators of old also used a technique that is useful in maintaining in your memory a speech or some other verbal declaration or declamation. This was called the walk, in which each part or point of their speech was linked by association to the various parts of their home, as would be viewed by them as they walked though it. For example, the entry way could be the preamble, and they could begin by stressing they were opening the door on a question or a mystery, and allowing light to enter into something previously concealed. This preamble could be elaborated on as desired, as the walk turned into the passage in the entryway, and the first point of the argument was revealed.

The goal of this technique is to make connections by association between the various items in the room and the various points you wish to make in the speech you are memorizing. This is the primary system Gordiano Bruno revealed in his famous book, 'The Art of Memory.' The system, of association by a walk is as valid today as it was in his time.

5

FINDING YOUR MAGIC NUMBER

~I~
From Your Inspiration

Sometimes a person will suddenly have a number come into their mind, and know that it is an important number for them. This number often has no connection to anything they may have been thinking of or considering. It may have no connection at all to anything in their life.

This number may just pop into the person's mind, suddenly being there for no reason at all. However, the number sticks with them, and they can't seem to get rid of it. This is gaining a number from your inspiration, which is one way of learning what your magic number is

No matter how it appears to you, and how it strikes you as being important, this number may not fit into any of the various number games you have ever heard of. It could be too large for the street number, or too far off for any of the other number games, seeming not to fit any of them. Yet, somehow, you know instinctively this is your number. One of the best ways to deal with that number, as once recommended to me by a famous numerologist, is to write it down and carry that number in you wallet or purse. It will bring you luck if you remember it and carry it with you.

~II~
Finding Your Magic Number
From Your Name And Birth Date

You may calculate your personal magic number from your name and birth date, as shown in the example below.

A – B – C – D – E – F – G – H – I - J - K- L- M- N- O – P - Q – R –S –T - U- V – W –X –Y – Z
1 – 2 – 3 – 4 – 5 – 6 – 7 – 8 – 9 – 10 – 11 – 12 – 13 – 14 – 15 – 16 – 17 – 18 – 19 – 20 – 21 – 22 – 23 – 24 – 25 - 26

Robert   Thomas   Collins

Robert = 18 + 15 + 2 + 5 + 18 + 20, which sums to 78

Thomas = 20 + 8 + 15 + 13 + 1 + 19, which sums to 76

Collins = 3 + 15 + 12 + 12 + 9 + 14 + 19, which sums to 84

Next we add in the birth date, which identifies this particular Robert Thomas Collins from all of the others who may be on this earth.

He was born on March 23, 1988 = 3 + 2 + 3 + 1 + 9+ 8 + 8, which sums to 34

To find the personal number of Mr. Collins, we must add all of these numbers together. This gives us: 78 + 76 + 84 + 34, which sums to 272

This is the personal magic number of that particular Mr. Robert Thomas Collins, who was born on the date given above, is 272. He should remember that number and carry it with him at all times. That number, when carried on his person, will act very much like a charm for him.

~III~
Finding Your Magic Number
From Playing Cards

Take a deck of ordinary playing cards, and separate them into the red and black suites. Men will use the black suits for finding their magic number, while women will use the red suites.

The values of the cards in these suits are as follows:
The Ace is equal to one. The 2 through 10 are the numbers shown on the card. A Jack is 11, while the Queen is 12, and the King is 13.

Now selecting either the red or black suites, shuffle the cards three times, or more. Men will now lay out three black cards selected from any part of the deck, without looking at them. A woman must lay out four red cards; again, she may select them from any part of the deck, also without looking at any of the cards.

Once the three or four cards have been selected, all of the remaining cads should be put away. This is to avoid the temptation to try again, if a card, or the final number, is not liked.

The person who has selected the cards now turns them over and adds up the numbers on the cards, as in the example below:

Three of clubs = 3 Queen of spades = 12 King of clubs = 13

This gives us 3 + 12 + 13, which sums to 28
The person who drew these cards now has that number, 28, as their magic number.

A woman might draw:

Five of hearts =5 Seven of diamonds = 7 Jack of hearts = 11 Ace of diamonds =1

This gives us 5 + 7 + 11 + 1, which sums to 24. This becomes her magic number.

~IV~

Blending The Influence Of All Of
Your Magic Numbers

Summing or adding all of the numbers you have found will give you a master number which you may use as you wish. As an example,

$$272$$
$$\underline{028}$$
$$300$$

This number may be used as a number to wager on the daily number or in whatever other way you desire to use it. A man I know signs his checks with his name, followed by his master number. He had won several nice sums from the lottery using his master number, so I suppose he is quite proud of it.

~V~

Making A Table Of Numbers Or
Keeping A Table Of Past Winning Numbers

If you are a dedicated lottery player you may want to keep a list of the winning numbers over the years. Those who have kept such a list for three or four years say there are some numbers which repeat often while there are others which just never seem to come up. If you know the numbers that come up often in a specific lottery, you will have an edge on the game. While if you are playing numbers that never come up, you must understand you are just feeding the kitty of your idle dreams.

I have been told there are lists of these numbers you can purchase on the Internet but I have not found any of them.

~VI~

Understanding The Numbers Games

Let us be honest about the lottery. Most lottery players loose their money. If you do not know for a fact you are one of the fortunate few players who consistently win, which means you win substantially more than you lose, you had best stop playing the lottery and look for a safer investment for your money. Remember, the people running the lottery, whether the street number or the sate number, don't do it for their health. They do it because they make money on it. They make money from those who lose much more than they win. Do your best to avoid being one of these losers.

~VII~
Putting Your Magic Numbers To Work

Playing the lottery is certainly one way to do so, and if you tend to be a fortunate person, it is probably a profitable way for you to use your magic numbers. If you are not someone who wins at the lottery, you will have to find other ways to use these numbers.

If you are getting a new telephone number you can ask the telephone company to give you a number that contains your magic numbers. In some areas they are most willing to do so, while in others they will require some convincing, but will still usually do so.

Locker numbers and street addresses often may be used with your magic number. A friend who teaches English told me that one of the better-known American writers uses his magic number in the residence address of his characters.

There are several ways to use your magic numbers. Try as many ways as you can. You may be surprised at the results you obtain.

6

GIVING MONEY TO ANCESTORS

The purpose of this spell must be to promote the well being of the deceased, as well as to establish funds for yourself. Insofar as you are able to focus upon enriching the ancestors you do this work for, so you will receive reciprocation from them in some manner.

The hell money that is mentioned here is available in most oriental grocery stores. A good-sized packet of this hell money usually costs about a dollar.

Take three pieces of Hell Money, and light them one at a time, saying the following prayer as you light each of the pieces of Hell Money in turn.

I address myself to ___Name___, my ___relationship___.

I give you money in death that you may increase your comfort, and so that you will assist me to have money in life.

Please send me money in excess, so that I may supply my daily needs and have excess money for luxuries.

MISCELLANY

I ask that you be comfortable in your death, and that God grant you peace.

Amen

Deceased parents and friends can all benefit from this work, and it will encourage them to benefit you in return. But you should do the work primarily for them, not for yourself.

You may perform this spell every month if you desire. It does seem to have beneficial results on the person who performs it, and the results are better if it is done regularly.

7

FOUR SPIRITUAL EXERCISES

These are not my exercises. I found them somewhere and decided to perform them. I worked with them for six months, and I am not sure if I became more spiritual as a result, but they certainly exposed to me a great deal of myself, including many parts of myself I had never faced before. As with all such exercises, I did not like what I discovered about myself, so I began correcting what I could. I recommend them to you in this same light. Work with them and try to rid yourself of what you find you do not like. Then work with them again. If you are conscientious in your efforts you will become a slightly better person as a result.

I have posted these exercises as I received them. As I recall, they were printed or typed on a single sheet of paper. Do not be deceived by their seeming simplicity they are a powerful set of exercises.

These exercises are to be repeated from time to time, until you have mastered them. They are to follow your having worked with the concentration and visualization exercises for at least six months. These exercises are each to be done for a month, alternating with a week or two without doing any of

MISCELLANY

these four exercises. The concentration and visualization exercises should be continued as these exercises are done, as well
as during the week or two you are resting.

(1) – For one month: Keep a record of the lies you have told.

(2) – Make a list of your spiritual expectations, or your spiritual
fantasies. Write the list out in detail, sparing nothing.

(3) – Identify your fears. With each fear, one at a time, ask
yourself, "Why do I fear this?" Over a month, work with one
fear a day and try to eliminate the fear from your being.

(4) – Every day for a month recall to yourself, "there is no such
thing as a meaningless or insignificant task."

8

LIFE IN THE CEMETERY

The graveyard is not really the quiet serene place it might seem to be to those who walk around it, possibly leaving flowers on the grave of a relative or friend. Among the many invisible spirits of the dead inhabiting the cemetery, we will find two main types, those who walk, and those who hide.

Those who hide are the spirits waiting patiently in their coffins, awaiting a resurrection that will never come, and losing energy as they lay waiting in their dreams, passing in non-physical life. Any spiritual force they may have engendered in their life – what people consider to be their souls - has already passed on, and is no longer connected to either the remains of their animal body or their animal driven emotional selves. What is left of these spirits, what we often refer to as the astral body, is fast passing away, as they gradually lose energy, whether reclining in the remains of their physical bodies or moving around in their non-physical bodies.

Immediately following the death of the physical body it has been said that the deceased enters into their beliefs. Those who believe in resurrection remain in their bodies, awaiting their resection and living in their self-created fantasies of the afterlife, which gradually fade away as their energy gradually decreases and disappears.

Those spirits called walking spirits have different interests. It frequently becomes an interest of the departing being to visit those with whom it feels an emotional connection. This is the source of those frequently reported apparitions of the newly deceased, appearing to their relatives and friends. These apparitions are actually very similar to the projection of the astral or non-physical bodies of the living, except in this case, there is nothing for the projected body to return to except the physical corpse. In the event the body has been cremated, there is not even that to use as it's housing.

There is some belief that the projected non-physical body may obtain energy from the corpse for at least the first few hours after the death of the body. This may be true, but the amount of energy available to the non-physical body depends greatly upon the vitality of the body when the person physically perished. A body from a strong and healthy person who perishes in an automobile accident is considerably more vital than that of someone who dies in bed after a long debilitating illness. The nature and process of death has a great deal to do with how much energy the non-physical body has left when death takes it.

Once the body is dead, and the non-physical body has taken all of the energy it can from the corpse, the non-physical body must operate on the remaining energy stored within it. There are several means of the non-physical body gaining energy, but as they are relatively unknown, it is unlikely the deceased will gain any additional energy following the demise of their physical shell. Their permanence as non-physical beings is usually dependent entirely on the energy they have stored within their non-physical bodies. In the majority of case, this is only enough energy for them to last in their non-physical bodies for a couple of years, at most. For those who die after a debilitating illness, there is usually even less energy available.

Once someone dies, they neither become enlightened nor do they increase their moral statue. Their character does not change, nor does the level of their education. This is why you will find among those who walk in the cemetery both those who are fundamentally good, and those who are fundamentally evil. The cemetery has a blend or cross section of society within it, even though they may be uniformly of their all holding to the same religion, or having the same professional or economic status.

Just as there are bullies in school, there are also bullies in the cemetery. Among those spirits who walk, there are often found those who wish to become the boss or dictator, and rule over the others. As with many other attempts of this sort, claiming power among the living, sometimes these bullies are able to take command of others, and sometimes they are not.

As there is a way in which a spirit may draw energy from other spirits, sometimes these negative or evil spirits may take command of the cemetery and rule it as their personal fiefdom for a great many years. This results in some of these cemeteries becoming essentially evil places, being placed under the control of evil spirits and their evil associates. New walking spirits coming into the cemetery must either subordinate themselves to these self appointed rulers of the graveyard, or depart. The wiser spirits depart immediately.

Prayers at the gate of the cemetery, or offerings made to the protector or guardian of the cemetery will often discourage these spirits from annoying the living. Some people are more the prey of negative spirits than are others. These people will often have problems visiting cemeteries. Most people interested in work with the dead, or learning these practices, will not have difficulty either entering a cemetery, doing work there, or buying dirt from graves.

Infrequently, a spirit may believe they have a cause against a person who is still alive. When this living person comes to the cemetery, the spirit may either afflict them or attach themselves to them. The living person may become aware of this, or they may not, depending on their own degree of sensitivity. Furthermore, it maybe possible to rid the living person of this difficulty or it may not. Again, this depends on the person's own degree of sensitivity, and the skill of the worker trying to rid them of the spirit.

9

GOOD AND EVIL – AN INTRODUCTION

Nothing presents a greater contrast between human and spiritual concepts as the ideas of good and evil held by incarnate human beings, and those ideas derived from the manifestations of the universal natural forces.

Human concepts of the nature of good and evil are promulgated by the particular religious and social system of the culture in which an individual is born and raised. In all formal religious practices there are definite ideas the theology of the religion holds dealing with what is good and what is evil. This set of theological concepts is developed into what may be considered as the moral laws the dominant religion of the culture seeks to have accepted by the civil authorities as the civil law of the land. In this way, the religious practice of the land becomes the 'Right Way,' to do things in the city, state, nation, or empire. Various religions attempt in many ways to explain why evil exists in the world that is frequently accepted as being otherwise good.

GOOD AND EVIL – AN INTRODUCTION

It is important to understand that all definitions of good and evil are social constructs, and as such, they are subject to change with time. These ideas of good and evil are also specific to locality and tradition. They are always defined in human terms, made to accord with what is believed to be good for a particular society or group of people. Man, for his own reasons, always devises these human definitions of what is good and what is evil. These human definitions rarely have any relationship at all to what is divinely ordained or universally true.

As with most things concerning this world of matter, mankind lives by rules that claim to be truth, but which are in fact only true for mankind in their relationship to the particular society in which they happen to live. Individuals need to realize these constructs have no real relationship to the unchanging truths of the universal reality.

The natural forces of the universe view good and evil as defined by mankind as human social constructs made for the human's own usage and pleasure. Mankind's view of good and evil is as different from the reality of the natural forces of the universe as is the truth of divinity from most human religious practices. In a few cases, human religious practices actually reveal what may be called a divine law. In the majority of cases, a vast gulf exists between what is truly divine and what humans consider to be divine. This gap is especially wide in terms of what is actually good and what is actually evil.

It is only at death, when the newly departed human soul enters the realm of the spirit, that the soul has the opportunity to review its actions over the course of a lifetime. It may then decide with the guidance of the spiritual forces the universe, whether the lifetime recently completed has been primarily a good life or primarily an evil life. This is the well-known 'Judgment of the Soul,' something that has been recognized and taught in many religions since the most ancient times.

Because of the false conceptions of good and evil that are taught by religions, government, and other social institutions, the newly departed soul is quite often surprised to discover in reviewing their life as seen from the spiritual viewpoint, and what they had perceived in their incarnate state.

The ultimate divine review of actions - judgments as to whether these actions are to be seen as good or evil – is based entirely on the evolution of the human soul involved. As a result, this judgment is always specifically situational, and is usually quite incomprehensible to the understanding of the average man. Naturally, this presents us with a quandary – How are we to judge our own actions? How are we to know if we are doing good or evil? Unfortunately, the answer is that we don't know. Only those who have obtained great spiritual merit have any idea as to whether their actions will result in what they might conventionally believe was either good or evil.

Because of this lack of true foreknowledge, people are simply urged to follow the codes of good and evil their society has defined and accepted. By behaving and acting in a socially conventionally good way, it is believed people will be forgiven any evil transgressions they might accidentally make. This seems to be true, as those who have been the exemplars of good in human history have urged this practice upon people since antiquity.

So if we wish to be good, and thereby obtain merit for ourselves, this is the course we should follow. At least we should seek to be conventionally good until we have obtained the great spiritual growth, the deep insight, needed to know the difference between what is actually good, and what is actually evil.

10

SOLVING PROBLEMS

The following is a sure fire way to solve problems of any kind. This method has worked for hundreds of people, some of whom have paid a couple of hundred dollars to learn this system. This system will work equally well for you, even though you are learning the secret for nothing.

FIRST – You have to understand that there are only three kinds of problems that a person can have in their life. Once you can understand and accept that, you have to decide which of these three kinds of problem you are really faced with. Take a moment and think it out calmly, as being emotional about it at this point will not solve the problem for you.

Is your problem:

> A Money Problem?
>
> A Health Problem?
>
> A Relationship Problem?

Problems are always either one of these three, or a combination of two of them. So, decide which one it is. If it's a combination of two of these, work on the one that is higher on the list above.

MISCELLANY

To solve your problem, permanently and effectively:

1.) - Write out exactly what your most pressing and serious problem is. Identify which of the three kinds of problems it is, or whether it might be a combination of two of them.

2.) – Now write out one word to describe exactly how you feel when you are thinking about that problem. Now it is time to bring your emotions into play and write out the word that describes how thinking about the problem makes you feel. It can be any word, but it will usually describe an emotion, such as miserable, anxious, hopeless, or fearful.

3.) – Now thinking about the problem again, write out one word describing how you would feel if you no longer had that problem. Again, use your emotions to describe how you would feel if the problem no longer existed. Think about this and make your decision. You will be choosing words that describe emotions, words like happy, satisfied, relieved, and free.

4.) – Next, turn away from the paper and take a deep breath. Pause and put all of this out of your mind. Now you know there are always ways to conquer this, and any other problem that may come into your life.

5.) – Next, turn back to the paper and make yourself feel the emotion you have written out as the answer to question three. Use your will power and force yourself to feel that emotion. You will consciously carry that emotion with you for the rest of the day, knowing that as you do so, the solution to the problem will present itself to you.

The same principles that make for a successful life make for a successful business. You can solve any problem you ever encounter with this sure fire method. It has worked for hundreds of people, and it will work for you.

11

WORKING WITH YOUR
NON-PHYSICAL BODY

In addition to all of the parts of your body you learned of as a child, and those internal parts you may have learned of as a medical practitioner, your body has a number of non-physical parts that you can use to your benefit, once you develop the ability to make use of them. Should you be certain that you do not have any non-physical body parts or appendages, you should stop right here, as you will not be able to develop the use of anything you do not, or cannot, recognize you have, or that it is possible for you to develop the use of.

Believing something can either be a benefit or a disadvantage to you in life. If you think you know something, it becomes impossible for you to learn anything about what you think you may know. It is always better to go through life with an attitude of childlike wonder, being open and willing to learn anything that may be presented to you.

Human beings are far more complex than their physical bodies reveal, as they have both physical and non-physical components. When you are a child, one of the purposes of play and games that you were encouraged to indulge in was to develop your physical body. Developing the non-physical parts of your body is a quite similar process, although with the non-physical, you must first identify the parts of your non-physical body, and then begin to understand and develop them.

We will begin with identifying your aura - that invisible part of you that surrounds you and is often referred to as your astral body, starry body, or non-physical body. We shall do this by the usual slow process of sure and certain development rather that trying for a fast but temporary identification, and then quickly moving on to something else.

Identifying Your Non Physical Body
Your Aura

1.) Wearing only your briefs, sit in a straight-backed chair in a dimly lighted room with your heels touching the two front rungs of the chair. Place your hands on your thigh, and relax yourself. Now breath with your diaphragm, taking slow and even breaths. Once you are comfortably relaxed, close your eyes and concentrate your attention on the surface of your skin.

2.) Notice that as you inhale, it seems as if your skin is contracting slightly, while as you exhale, it seems as if your skin is reaching out, or expanding somehow. Passively observe this effect for a few moments as you continue to breath slowly and regularly.

3.) Once you have observed this effect for a while, see yourself expand out of your skin as you exhale, and return to your skin as you inhale. Try and see yourself project out an inch or two from your body as you exhale, and then return to the surface of your skin as you inhale. You may open your eyes and see if you can notice this effect. Most people cannot see anything at all, so don't be disappointed if you see nothing. Some people see what they refer to as heat waves, while other people say they see a moving line. If you see something, that's nice, otherwise be unconcerned and continue to feel the expansion and contraction. Continue to practice this exercise for a few moments every day, then get up and go about your daily affairs. Repeat this exercise every day for several weeks until you can identify your aura without any doubt or hesitation. Once you can identify you aura, this is a good exercise to practice as you dress in the morning.

4.) The next exercise may be practiced any time you wish. I have found it is something worthwhile doing while riding on public transportation. Look at your hands, and as you inhale feel the energy around your hands. Feel this energy expanding slightly as you exhale. You do not have to make any kind of show about this, just look at your hands as you breath. You may do this any time you wish, for as much time as you have to devote to it. You should do this exercise as long as you are doing the other astral exercises, as it will be of great assistance to you in developing your ability to sense your non-physical body.

It might be of interest to learn that your aura does actually expand and contract with every breath. This happens naturally, whether you are aware of it or not. The purpose of these exercises is to make you consciously aware of this natural phenomenon.

What you are doing with these exercises is attempting to become consciously aware of the non-physical effect of your aura expanding and contracting with your breathing. As you do this, you are becoming aware of your non-physical aura. In time you will be able to sense your non-physical body as a part of yourself, recognizing it as easily as you recognize your arms and legs.

If you are going to learn to project your non-physical or astral body, you must begin by learning to be familiar with it. If you master the above exercises, you will gain conscious familiarity with your non-physical body. You should practice these excises until you can attune your physical body to your non-physical aura any time you wish.

Once you have attuned yourself to recognizing you aura, and are familiar with it, you may go into deliberately expanding and shrinking your aura. For this exercise you should put yourself in the same position as you were for the first exercise. You should be comfortably seated on a straight back chair in a dimly lighted room.

MISCELLANY

1.) Relax yourself and breathe slowly with your diaphragm. Now take a deep breath and feel your aura expanding out away from your body. Inhale and hold the air in your lungs. Then exhale while holding your aura out and away from your body. Inhale while maintaining you aura out and away from your body. Hold your aura out and away from your body as you breath in and out several times. Then deliberately contract your aura as you consciously visualize your aura contracting to your body.

Do this exercise three or four times at each opportunity, at least once a day. Once you believe you have mastered this exercise, continue to practice it at least once a day for another month. This exercise will help you to develop conscious control over your astral body, which is so necessary to successful astral projection.

2.) Next, in the same position, project a part of yourself. For example, lift your non-physical hand from your thigh, separating it from your physical hand and arm. Now hold your non-physical hand and arm out in front of you. Then replace your non-physical hand in the position it was before, and do the same exercise with the other hand and arm. This exercise can be done once you believe you have mastered the first exercise in this series. Then you can do both of the exercises together, until you are able to feel your non-physical hand and arm as well as your physical hand and arm.

If you cannot feel your physical hand and arm when you have extended your non-physical hand and arm, do not be concerned. Some people can feel their non-physical body, while others cannot. Either way is perfectly normal.

3.) Once you believe you have mastered the above exercise, begin to open and close your non-physical fingers, when your non-physical hand and arm are extended in front of you. Practice making a fist and releasing it with your non-physical hand, as your physical hand remains resting on your thigh, not moving at all. You should also rotate your wrist, and otherwise move your non-physical hand as you have your non-physical hand and arm extended in front of you.

Practice this exercise with both hands, until you are certain you can manipulate your non-physical hands and arms as well as you can manipulate your physical hands and arms. Mastering this exercise often takes a great deal of time, effort, and practice. Do not be in a hurry to move on, but master all of these exercises as well as you can before you move on to the next exercise.

4.) Practice lifting your non-physical legs and manipulating them as you did with your arms and hands. Again, take your time and begin by working with one leg at a time until you have gained the control you need. Move or manipulate your feet and ankles in the same way you manipulated your non-physical wrists.

5.) Combine the above two exercises so that you can manipulate both your non-physical hands and feet while your physical hands and feet remain in a fixed position. Once you have mastered these exercises you are ready to go further.

PARTS OF THE NON-PHYSICAL BODY
The Invisible Hand

Sitting on your straight chair, and wearing only your briefs, measure one thumb knuckle's distance beneath your navel. The first knuckle of your thumb, of the hand you write with, should rest at the base of your navel opening, the thumb pointing down toward your crotch. Now mark the point at the tip of your thumb with a marker of some kind, like an erasable pen or a Sharpie pen. A small dot is sufficient; you just need to know where this point is. Once you have that point marked, and have located it in your mind, just relax, but focus your attention on that point on your body.

1.) Close your eyes, and breathing slowly and evenly, feel this point of your body extend itself like a serpent or a hand, expanding and contracting as you inhale and exhale. Don't get fancy at this point, just feel it extending out and retracting into your body again. This point of your body, an organ of your non-physical body, is known as the Invisible Hand, the Searching Hand, or the Helping Hand.

You should add this exercise to your daily exercise routine and gradually continue extending and retracting your Invisible Hand until you feel you can sense it along its entire length. Once you can consistently feel the entire extended length of your invisible hand, you can begin having your invisible hand touch walls, the floor, and other surfaces.

Unlike your physical hand and arm, your invisible hand may be extended to any length you may desire. Thus, once you have mastered its use, you can extend your invisible hand to touch something across a room, or in the far corner of the ceiling.

Take your time with this, as the sensations you will receive when touching something you are familiar with using your invisible hand will not be the same as when you touch something with your physical hand. Once you can identify and touch whatever you wish in the room you are in, you can go on to the next exercise.

2.) Bring a small table, like a card table, in the room with you and put a variety of things on top of it, a sheet of paper, several coins of different sizes or denominations, a pen, a pencil, a dish with some water in it, and a book you have read (thus one that has your mental impressions on it).

Relax yourself, and close your eyes. Now extend your invisible hand and guide it to the card table. If you can do this without opening your eyes, just by sensing the 'vibrations' or sensations in the room, you are doing very well indeed. Once you have found the card table, back off and find it again. Do this until you can consistently locate the card table with your invisible hand. You are searching for the blend of impulses that are provided by the card table and the assortment of things you have placed on it. Please master this exercise before going any further. You should practice this exercise every day for at least a week or two. It will take at least that long to master it.

WORKING WITH YOUR NON PHYSICAL BODY

As you might expect, the next step is sensing the individual objects on the card table. You must have mastered the previous step to be able to learn this next one.

3.) Project your invisible hand to the card table. Now open your eyes and will the invisible hand to touch the sheet of paper. You will touch it all over, but begin at one corner and trace the outside of the paper before going to the middle of the paper. Mastering this may take a bit of time, as you are developing your ability to fine control the motions of your invisible hand.

Gradually touch all the other objects on the table, learning the difference between the sizes of the coins and the dimensions of the book. Spend time on this, as mastering the control of your invisible hand, and being able to recognize shapes, sizes, and dimensions is very important. Not only feel the bowl you have placed on the table with a little water in it, but touch the water in the bowl as well. This is to give you the sensation of learning what wet feels like with your invisible hand. It will feel differently from the way water feels wet when you touch it with your physical hand.

When you were a child you had to learn what things you could touch, and what things you should not touch. You also had to learn what dimensions were and what colors were. I am sure you did not learn all these things overnight. Mastering these things took you some time. You will have made errors, and you will have had successes on the way to this mastery. Just as it took you time to master your contact with the physical universe, it will take you some time to master sensing and identifying things with your invisible hand. You are learning how to master contact with the invisible universe. Don't be impatient. Take your time. Master each step of the process along the way, as you are developing a very important tool for your use.

Breathing With Your Skin

Learning to breath with your skin can keep your skin younger looking and more flexible as you age. This is accomplished in much the same manner as identifying your aura. However, this time we will be concentrating on sensing and feeding the physical rather than the non-physical.

Focus your attention on your left forearm as you sit as described previously in your straight-backed chair, and are normally relaxed. Feel your arm taking in energy with every breath. Spend a minute or two on this, and then do the same with your right forearm. Now look at one of your feet, and do the same, visualizing your foot taking in energy with every breath. Then repeat this with the other foot. Spend about five minutes on this exercise every day. This will be a good exercise for you to use to finish off your daily exercise session.

In time, and as you feel more confident, extend this visualization to your hands, your ankles, your lower legs, and thighs. You will be able to extend this exercise to your entire body over time. Once you have mastered this exercise, and are doing it every day, you will begin to notice slight changes in your skin. The first apparent changes are usually faster healing from cuts, scrapes, scratches, and bruises, as well as noticing more resiliency and flexibility of your skin. The changes are more noticeable in people who are forty or older than they are in the very young, but the changes are present never the less. Continue this exercise until you can breathe with the skin of your whole body. Then breathe like this for about three to five minutes at least four or five times a week, to maintain the skin health you have obtained. Even very old people can benefit from this exercise. In the case of the aged, the changes in their skin are often quite remarkable.

Exerting Force With Your Non Physical Body

Let me say at the beginning, this is a very difficult exercise, and not everyone can master it. If you have not mastered the previous exercises, it is unlikely you will be able to master this one. Concentrate on this exercise, and work at it, but while the effort you make will be of benefit to you, you may not ever be terribly successful at it. Don't be disappointed just do the best you can, but please work at it for at least a year before abandoning this exercise.

Balance a playing card on the edge of a book so that the slightest disturbance or effort will knock it off. Test this, knocking the card off with the touch of a feather, or a puff of breath. Then sit in your straight chair, relax yourself, and try to knock the card off the book with your invisible hand. Deliberately try to knock the card off the book three times, then rest and go on to practice another exercise. Be patient. As I say, this is a very difficult exercise for anyone to master.

Should you be able to master knocking the card off your book, you should go on to knocking off a domino balanced on the book. If you are successful, you can go on to working with moving a number of even heavier objects. Try pushing a domino around the card table. Putting the domino on a sheet of paper will make it a little easier. Rolling a marble is a good beginning test before you try pushing the domino. The ultimate test of this art is being able to lift something with your invisible hand. A few people have been known to be able to do this.

Projecting Your Thoughts

Projecting your thoughts is not telepathy; it is a matter of sending your thoughts out into the vast universe. Its relationship to telepathy might be compared to that of a small explosion in an empty desert to a sniper's accurate rifle shot. Please do not believe that mastering this exercise will give you the ability to command others, or even to communicate with others. It will just allow you to project your thought out into the universe when you desire to do so.

Consciously and deliberately form a brief thought on the third eye region of your forehead. This is directly above your nose, and about centered top to bottom on your forehead. Focus all of your attention on that thought, and then take three deep breaths, willing the breaths to energize that thought. Now move the thought up and across the top of your head, and down to the base of your skull. Once it is there, release it.

Do not think of that thought; do not be concerned with where it goes, or with what happens to it. Let it go. Thinking about the thought will either ground it, or call it back to you again. This is exactly what you do not want to happen.

The more brief the thought you project, the greater impact it will have. A thought of four words will have about half the impact of a thought of two words, although this comparison is not entirely accurate, as the words you use also need to be considered. Just understand this is a technique that is teaching you something. Once you master this technique, you will have developed a useful ability that may be expanded upon later on.

Gaining Familiarity With Parts Of Your Visible and Invisible Bodies

The less sexually inhibited or physically modest you are the better this exercise will work for you. Most people accept their body, often disliking parts of it, but they never really take the time to become truly familiar with the various parts of their physical body. You should take the time to thoroughly examine your body, using a full-length mirror, and a hand mirror. Study your body carefully, and see just what you think of every part of it. Be as objective as possible, and note your emotional reactions to the various parts of your body as you examine it.

Which parts of your body do you believe are attractive? Which parts of your body do you not like, or may even repulse you? You should note all of this information down, as it will actually be valuable to you later on when we begin exploring your non-physical body in some detail.

If you can do so, place your straight-backed chair in front of a floor length mirror, and sit in it, looking into the mirror. Observe yourself breathing, and watch yourself as you relax your physical body. Study your body in as objective a manner as you can achieve, in the same way you might study a painting or a sculpture. Make note of any thoughts you may have concerning your body, whether they are critical or complimentary.

Use a hand mirror to inspect the parts of your body you cannot easily see. Stand up, and look in to the floor length mirror. Place one foot at a time on the chair and look into the mirror, studying your body, inspecting it.

The object of this exercise is to get you completely familiar with your physical body. Once you have examined every part of your body, you should sit in your straight back chair, and recall what the various parts of your body looked like. Until you can recall the appearance of your hands and feet, navel, arms and legs, you have not mastered this exercise. This is not as simple an exercise as it may initially seem to be. So examine yourself carefully and in detail every day for at least a couple of weeks to understand that you have to gain familiarity with the appearance of your physical body. Once you can recall what you look like all over your body, you will have mastered this exercise.

Your non-physical body will look very much the same as your physical body, as it is contained inside it. However, as we have seen, your non-physical body has features your physical body does not have, such as your invisible hand. If you have been visualizing the arms and legs of your non-physical body extending out of your physical arms and legs, you may have discovered that you can bend your non-physical arms and legs into positions you cannot bend your physical arms and legs. For example, you can completely revolve your non-physical hands and feet without any strain or difficulty. I do not recommend you do this often, but it is something for you to keep in mind.

Exerting Force With Your Non-Physical Hands

Once you have mastered knocking a playing card off the book with your invisible hand, there is another exercise you can learn, which is at least equally difficult. Place a ping-pong ball on a smooth table. Sit at the table, with your physical hands on your thighs, and try to roll the ping-pong ball back and forth with your non-physical hands. You may find your physical hands tingle or move slightly as you do this, but pay no attention to them, concentrate on your non-physical hands, and try to roll the ping-pong ball back and forth. If the ball suddenly rolls off the table, get it and resume the exercise with it. Once you have mastered this, use a tennis ball, and then a baseball. If you have had problems knocking the playing card off the book, you can go back to it once you have begun trying to move the ping-pong ball, whether you have been successful with it or not. You will find you will be far more successful in using your invisible hand.

The same procedure is used to develop the ability to exert force with your non–physical feet. Sitting on your straight-backed chair, on a smooth floor, try and kick a ping-pong ball with your non-physical foot. Alternate kicking, first using one foot, and then another. Once you have mastered using your non-physical hands with the ping-pong ball, you are well on your way to mastering using your feet as well.

It is entirely possible to separate the various non-physical parts of your body, and apply them separately or together to various useful tasks. Once you believe you have mastered this art, you can practice this on a train or bus. If you use your non-physical hand to reach out and tickle the ear of someone across the aisle from you and up a few seats, you will usually notice them react, as if a fly had teased them. Do this with someone who it is physically impossible for you to reach. This will avoid any suspicion falling on you. Not everyone will appreciate your playfulness in learning and mastering this art.

As with anything else, constant practice develops the ability.

The Indications Of Your Physical Body

Your physical body reveals certain things about you. These are things that will influence and guide your life, whether you believe they will or not. Once you understand these indications, you will be able to harmonize yourself with them and cease fighting against the destiny that has been provided for you, whatever it may be.

Hair – The Hair on your head is indicative of your natural religiosity, or your faith in a supreme being. Those who lose their hair at an early age, say before they are fifty are said to have little natural religiosity. Course hair on the head is said to relate to those of a course nature while fine hair is said to reveal those of a more refined nature. The presence or lack of religiosity might be said to apply to those who lose their hair after fifty, except this seems to relate more to the amount of testosterone in their system. Those with high levels of testosterone seem to lose the hair on their heads, while those with less testosterone seem to keep it.

The amount of body hair is said to relate to the animal nature of the person, those of a more animal nature having more body hair. Some people, of both sexes, are complexly covered in body hair, while other people have very little hair on their bodies, or have only very short fine body hair. This may be more genetic than spiritual however, as there are American Indians who have abundant hair on their heads, and very little or no body hair at all.

The Breasts – Breasts indicate the supportive and nutritive feature of the individual. Prominent breasts on the nude body indicate someone who is able to be supportive and nurturing of another. While this is said to apply to both men and women, in a woman, their B or C cup breast indicates the desire to be nurturing of others.

The Nipples – The proportional difference between the length and diameter of your nipples indicate your biological sexual demand, the amount of sexual contact your biological system desires to have. The longer your nipples are in proportion to their diameter, the greater your biological sexual demand. The diameter of the nipple is measured and divided into the length of the nipple. The greater the ratio, the greater the biological sexual demand of the person.

Women who are born with a naturally sexually promiscuous nature may have nipples that are two or three times longer than their diameter, or infrequently even longer. Their urge for frequent and widespread sexual contact is a part of their divinely intended nature, and may not safely interfered with, or held back by so-called human morality.

MISCELLANY

The Thumbs – The ratio between the first and second joint of your thumb indicate the ratio between the thought and the will power you put into making and acting upon decisions. The first joint, from fingertip beneath the nail to the knuckle, is emblematic of your willpower, while the second joint is emblematic of your thought. Ideally, the two are equally balanced.

Those people who have a very large first joint, showing a great degree of will power with little underlying thought, are referred to as having a murderers thumb. This is because they often take action without sufficient prior thought. Those people who have very short first thumb joints, compared to their second joints, tend to think too much before acting, often delaying or postponing any action at all. It should be apparent that either condition might lead to a personal disaster for the person.

The ability to form a right angle with the thumb and the first finger is said to be a sign of mechanical ability in a person.

Woman's Hips – It has been known for centuries that those women with wide hips have an easier time in childbirth. However, despite the widespread idea that wide hips indicate fertility in women, this is just not so. Women with narrow hips often have to undergo cesarean section in order to successfully deliver children. One of the reasons for delaying sexual intercourse with women until they have reached physical maturity is to allow them to develop their full growth, and thus their greatest hip dimensions.

Calf To Ankle Ratio – The ratio of the calf to the ankle of a person is a reasonably accurate indicator of their general intelligence. The diameter of the calf at its largest point versus the diameter of the ankle at its smallest point set this ratio. The greater the ratio, or basically, the smaller the ankle diameter, the more intelligent the person is judged to be.

The above information is just an indication of the well-known idea that the human body contains within it an indication of the person's destiny, as well as providing a message of guidance for the person. Obviously the above material just scratches the surface of this information.

WORKING WITH YOUR NON PHYSICAL BODY

Once you can understand your physical body contains signs of benefit to you, I believe you can also understand you non-physical body contains similar signs. To go one step further, it is possible for a specialist in what is known as physical astrology to reconstruct your complete natal horoscope from their close examination of your physical body. Each mark, blemish, mole, or spot on your physical body has meaning to the one able to make the proper deductions from them. As this is a specialist matter, I am very soon out of my depth in attempting to explain this art, but I will mention that astrology divides the body from the head, said to be ruled by Aries, to the feet, said to be ruled by Pisces. Most astrology books have information on this, or at least an illustration depicting it.

The Color Of Your Aura

There are people who naturally see colors in the auras of those around them. Some people see all kinds of things in the aura, diagrams, symbols, crowns, and wings. Most people look at another person and see nothing at all. There are special glasses that supposedly allow one to view the aura of another. Invented by a London hospital electrician, he used them to successfully diagnose illnesses in the bodies of those he viewed. Naturally, the medical establishment soon put a stop to that.

Should you be fortunate enough to be able to see the aura of another person, you should do your best to learn as much about the aura you view as you can. However, do not attempt to diagnose illness in another person, as this is a criminal act in most legal jurisdictions of the world. When I see someone who has an illness either at the time or manifesting in the immanent future, I will only suggest they visit a physician for a thorough physical examination. If I see their death within a year or two I only suggest they make out a will. I suggest you adopt a similar policy.

I believe in allowing the professions to have their due, as there is a terrible karmic price to be paid for the actions of many of those professionals who believe they are helping others. The same applies to those who are working in charitable organizations, religious missions, and generally doing what they believe are good works. A machinist has a better chance of gaining spiritual advancement from their work than someone who feeds a thousand poor children a day for several years. This is just an example of the fact that what mankind believes to be good is in fact often evil, while what he believes to be evil is in fact, often good.

Feeding Your Aura

Indigo blue, whether in a food grade dye or from indigo blue balls aids in strengthening the aura. The best procedure is to us the blue coloring in soaking baths. In extreme cases, clothes may be soaked in indigo blue water and placed on the person's body. Do not expect miraculous cures from this practice, as it takes time for the aura to wear down, so it will take time for the aura to build up again. In the case of extreme tiredness and auric difficulties, daily bathes in indigo blue solution are advised. A series of seven or nine baths is recommended. In less extreme cases, five baths taken on alternate days is advised.

12

CANDLE MAGIC PROSPERITY SPELLS

THE GREEN CANDLE MONEY SPELL

This spell is taken from the work of Ms. Catherine Ponder of the Unity Church who wrote several books about gaining prosperity several years ago.

The spell requires a green candle, a red pen, and a piece of paper. Money Drawing Oil may be used to dress the candle if desired.

Write the dollar amount of money you need in the center of the paper with a red pen, indicating what the money is to be used for. You should also mention that you intend to a make charitable contribution of some kind with part of the money.

Dress the candle with money drawing oil if you wish, then place it in its holder. Place the candleholder over the paper you have written the amount you need on. Sincerely pray over the candle that you receive the money you desire, and as you pray, light the candle. Once you have finished your prayer, allow the candle to burn out.

That's all there is to it. This is the simplest money spell there is. Try it, as it has been quite successful for many people.

THREE CANDLE MONEY SPELL

AL H Morrison BA, who told me it paid his rent every month since he began doing it for his friends, gave me this spell. I have used it successfully for several of my students who were in financial difficulties.

This well-known spell should only be done once if you are doing it for yourself. It may be done three times if you are doing it for someone else.

When you have completed the spell, do not think about it. Especially do not think about, or decide, from which direction, or how, the money will come to you. These thoughts tend to limit the spell severely, often denying you, or the person you have prayed for, the money that is rightfully theirs.

Take three candles, they may be regular white candles of any size, but if they are colored, one should be white, one green, and one purple. Place them in three candleholders, and set them in a row in front of you as you perform this spell.

Now have matches to hand, and relax yourself a bit and prepare yourself for the spell. If you have colored candles, (not a necessity) the purple candle should be on the left, the green in the middle, and the white candle on the right.

Now light the left most candle, and pray that your income and the source of your income be protected against all adversity.

Then wait a moment until the flame of that candle stabilizes.

Light the center candle with a prayer that your income increase to the amount you desire, (Selecting a reasonable amount, one within your sphere of availability.)

Again, wait a moment or two until the flame stabilizes.

Finally, light the right most candle, praying that you use the money you will receive wisely, and to the good of all of the people concerned in your life.

Allow all three of the candles to burn completely out. If you are doing this spell for someone else, it should be done three times, on three consecutive days, and the candles burned out each time. You should not use long burning or seven-day candles, although it might be tempting to do so.

Once again, when the spell is finished, put it completely out of your mind.

13

ASKING SOMEONE FOR A FAVOR

Have you ever asked someone to do you a favor?

Perhaps you wanted them to pick something up for you, or let you leave work early? These are all things we may need to have accomplished for us by others. Asking other people to do us favors is just another part of our ordinary daily life.

Normally, if you are helpful to others, doing them small favors when they ask, you will find they will be happy to reciprocate, doing favors for you when you ask. This is the social-psychological principle of reciprocation, in which people seek to balance out favors done them, by doing favors for others in return. Thus, when you ask someone you have done a favor for to reciprocate, they will usually do so, if it is possible for them to do so.

Benjamin Franklin in his autobiography pointed out that if you wished to make a friend of anther man, asking the other man to do you a small favor would go a long way toward beginning the process of establishing your favorable relationship with them. He suggested borrowing a book from the man you wished to befriend you. It should be obvious that you must return the book once you have read it.

ASKING SOMEONE FOR A FAVOR

In this case, you put yourself in debt to the other person, so by the social rule of reciprocation, you owe them a similar favor in the future.

If you ask a number of people to fulfill a request you make, you are likely to find no one will respond to your request. This is caused by another social-psychological principle, the diffusion of responsibility. Here, each of the people you are broadcasting your request to believe that someone else will "take care of it." In this case, the group of people you ask are now emotionally freed from the social responsibility of reciprocation.

How can you be certain that someone will step forward to fulfill your request, doing you the favor you wish to have accomplished? Firstly, you should always be certain you are asking the individual in person for the favor, not asking them as members of a group, no matter how well defied that group is. For example, asking someone personally is always better than asking a group of people you have done favors for in the past.

Secondly, you should be specific as to just what the favor or request you are asking then for is. "Please buy me a Hershey bar, here's the money," is far better than "Bring me back something for me from the store."

Thirdly, you should always ask first the person you believe will be most likely to say yes to your request. If they are unable to be of assistance, then you may directly ask the next most likely person, and so forth.

Fourthly, be sure you are asking for something that is both reasonable and possible for the person you are asking to accomplish. Asking the difficult or the impossible is more likely to gain you a laugh than a favorable response from the person you asked.

Following these rules will insure you will have most of your requests for favors fulfilled by others.

14

RELIGION

Generally speaking, religion is a useful force for social control. It tends to make a population uniform in their beliefs, and behave correctly in this world, in hopes of a better life to come in the next world, or often promising another and better physical life after physical death, as most religions tend do. Thus all religions hold out theoretical hopes for the future, and do their best to ease the pangs and perversities of the present.

In fact, no religion has any real idea of what comes after human death, or of what system of rewards and punishment (If any) might be applied following such a transition. Of course, once the transition is accomplished the newly deceased has no means of complaint against those who so deliberately lied to them to earn their keep.

As there can never be any opposition in fact to the beliefs promulgated about the world after death, religion becomes a very powerful force for insuring social uniformity. However, like all other powerful forces found in this world, fire, and government among them, religion must be applied carefully and with great caution.

RELIGION

The Roman Emperor Constantine, usually credited with being the prime force behind Christianity, wished to use one religion in the empire to insure unanimity of belief in the populace. He began this great effort, but was unable to complete his work until well after the Roman Empire itself had crumbled into dust, and only the Roman Universal Church, the product of his foundation, remained.

The Roman Church provided a uniform belief all through Europe, which was not effectively challenged until the lack of arms of the church, along with the Church's greed for wealth, forced the Germanic nobility to turn to Luther as their source of religious wisdom. It was the protest against increased religious taxation by the church, and not a protest against the Roman Catholic religion that made the protestant (or protesters) church, the norm in North Germany, and eventually brought Lutheranism, and later Protestantism, as we know it today, into the world.

In fact, the more religious a society is, the more criminal, and the more divergent from any law-abiding ideal it becomes. The lifestyle of the middle ages, if honestly investigated, shows this. This lifestyle was not damped by the protestant reformation; but was only halted by the industrial revolution and the growth of social and economic power in the laboring class through trade and industrial unionization. This has been shown time and time again by statistical analysis, although this is one of those demonstrable truths, which "everyone just knows to be false."

The more any religion permeates a society, especially at the lower level, the more tractable people may appear to be, but the higher the incidence of dementia, delusion, and general mental malaise will be found. The only true solutions to this is that those with the greatest delusional or malignant commitment to the state religion be removed from society and institutionalized promptly, preferably as soon as any signs of their mental difficulty is bought to light. This requires a true and full separation of the church and state.

Fanaticism, and most especially religious Fanaticism, is always to be treated as a severe mental condition, one worthy of permanent institutionalization. Belief in a religion of any kind is to be discouraged among those who are the providers of the various religious services to the public. Those who have very strong faith in religion are bearing all of their weight upon a fragile stick, and should that stick ever bend or break, as it often will, their individual sanity will pass away with their faith in the stick they have over stressed. Thus, at the least, these providers of religious propaganda and service to the masses must be carefully watched with an eye to removing them should their mental load begin to become so great their minds start to crack.

A wide diversity of religions, especially proselizing religions, in any culture always leans toward strife and confusion. A uniformity of religion always leads toward bigotry and mental oppression in the populace. Religion is always something that must be taken in very small doses, and not ever thought to be anything of primary importance in the daily life of the person.

Indifference to religion is the best practice in any culture, along with the firm control of those who claim that to preach any religion is their right.

15

MAGIC WITH WORD AND NUMBER SQUARES

The Theory And Practice
Of Working Magic With Word And Number Squares

The concept of working magic with word and number squares is based on the animist idea that there is a non-physical spirit or 'intelligence,' of some kind connected to each of the particular squares being used. This spirit or intelligence is thought to be intrinsic to each of the many possible word or number squares. The squares and spirits are individualized in such a way that the square may be used to call or summon the specific spirit connected to that combination of words, letters, or numbers used in forming the square. The spirit may then be asked to perform whatever work is in the nature or the domain of the spirit connected to that particular square. Fortunately, most 'magic squares,' of whatever type, reveal their domain of influence in the written description that accompanies them, either in the text of the book in which they occur or otherwise. Alternatively, you could call (summon) the spirit of the square and ask it what it might be interested in doing for you, although this is usually believed to be a less certain way of working, but it is most likely the way the descriptions of the squares found in books were originally obtained.

The magic squares of the seven major planets of antiquity are well known, and have been repeatedly published all over the world. As a result, there is a rather large thoughtform that may be used in dealing with each of them. This large and powerful thoughtform acts to encourage, and practically assure, the opportunity of success for the person who uses these planetary magic squares to assist them in casting spells relating to the rulership of the planetary spirits.

We have, for example, the magic square of Saturn, which is used for restriction, confinement, negation, coagulation, concretion, and all of the many other aspects of the affairs of Saturn.

```
8 1 6   6 1 8   4 9 2   2 7 6   2 9 4
3 5 7   7 5 3   3 5 7   9 5 1   7 5 3
4 9 2   2 9 4   8 1 6   4 3 8   6 1 8    etc.
```

These variations are all the same magic square, as can be seen by inspection. How many other varieties of this magic square can you make from these numbers? Are all of these variations connected to the same non-physical planetary influence? It would take some experimentation to learn the truth of this, would it not? However, it is certainly an idea for the experimentation of an interested magician.

One of the best-known letter squares used in Magic is the famous SATOR Square. It has been used for everything from a medical aid, to a domestic fire extinguisher. This square had been found everywhere, from inscriptions on walls and lead plates in ancient Rome, all through the Middle Ages, where it was used for a wide variety of purposes, to the present day.

In parts of medieval Germany, this square was once used as a fire extinguisher. Homeowners were required to have a prepared square on hand, usually painted on a wooden disk or platter. It was to be cast into a burning building to put the fire out.   Naturally, there is some question as to whether these magic squares actually worked for that purpose.

However, the Sator square has not lost its charm; it is presently included in a variety of modern day magician's books. This square has certainly had a long and varied career. Even today it is said that the house that has this square placed in the center of the building, and at its highest point, need never fear damage from fire.

Used primarily against conflagration, The Sator Square has also been used in everything from love spells to sealing prayerful letters pleading for assistance from the creator. It is certainly one of the oldest and best known of all magic letter squares. This ancient magic square is still in everyday use today. Many people still believe it is quite effective as a preventative against fire or other disaster.

S A T O R
A R E P O
T E N E T
O P E R A
R O T A S

Aside from squares, there are also a number of other letters and number arrangements used both in the practice of magic, and in 'traditional,' or folk healing arts. One example of these is the ABRACADABRA triangle used for some centuries to decrease fevers in both children and adults. The triangle is carefully and prayerfully written out on paper, with the intention that as the letters disappear, one at a time, so the fever will also disappear. The completed triangle is placed on the child or adult, often by using a string to tie it around the neck with the point of the square aimed down. When it is used in this way, the fever is supposed to be gone by morning. The fever is supposed to gradually fade away, just as the letters of the word disappear one at a time.

MISCELLANY

```
ABRACADABRA
 ABRACADABR
  ABRACADAB
   ABRACADA
    ABRACAD
     ABRACA
      ABRAC
       ABRA
        ABR
         AB
          A
```

A similar triangle used both as a medical preventative and for healing, is expansive rather than diminishing. This triangle is said to work effectively against blindness, so the triangle itself increases, allowing the sight of the person who uses it to increase over time. As with the former triangle, the following one is to be prayerfully written out on paper and affixed to the clothing of the afflicted person. It may be written small and placed as a charm on the person who has poor eyesight or on someone who is developing cataracts. They are expected to wear it for some time, so the charm may have to be replaced should it wear out or become damaged in some way.

This charm is not as popular as the Abracadabra charm, possibly because it is not as well known.

```
S
SC
SCH
SCHI
SCHIA
SCHIAU
SCHIAUR
SCHIAURI
SCHIAURIR
SCHIAURIRI
```

MAGIC WITH WORD AND NUMBER SQUARES

Probably the best-known repository of word and number squares used for magic is the book 'The Sacred Magic of Abramelin the Mage,' better known as 'The Book of Abramelin.' This book is available in two translations, an incomplete one made by S. L. MacGregor Mathers, in the nineteenth century, and a new, more complete and more accurate rendition from George Dehn and Steve Guth, published in 2006 by Ibis Press in Florida. The whole book of Abramelin consists of four books, only three of which were translated by Mathers from the abbreviated French manuscript he found in the Library of the Arsenal. The explanation, the folk spells, and the initial theurgic work do not concern us here, as we are only concerned with the word and number squares, which are given in the fourth book. According to the author, these squares are useful in summoning the spirit to which the squares are connected.

The theurgic work, given in the third book which takes eighteen months to complete, is done to have another spirit, or even several spirits, become attached to the magician, both for his assistance and his guidance.

While many of these letter and number squares are balanced letter constructions, like the Sator Square, not all of the word squares of the Abramelin book are constructed in such a balanced manner. Some squares seem to be made of mixed or possibly random letters, having an unknown source. The meaning of the words used in these squares, if in fact they are words, is obscure at best. While the original language of the Abramelin book was German, it is quite possible that the letter squares were originally written in Hebrew, Arabic, or some other unknown language. Some of these squares may have a more ancient provenance than even the fifteenth century origin claimed for the original Book of Abramelin.

There seems to be a generally understood belief that the letter and number squares in the book of Abramelin may not be used correctly by anyone who has not undergone the eighteen month theurgic preparation, and through that attained the Knowledge and Conversation of their Holy Guardian Angel, which is the object of this long theurgic operation.

Another, and possibly more rational way to put this is that people will not be able to gain from the use of these squares unless they have been able to demonstrate some competence and ability in the practice of magic in other forms. I would say that this latter is more probably correct. Using squares of letters and numbers is only another form of the art of magic. It is certainly not the only form.

A very small sample of the many squares found in the Abramelin book include:

```
M O R E H
O RI RE
R I N I R
E RI R O
H E R O M
```

Square One, Book One, Chapter One, 'To Know Past Things'

We shall balance this square with the succeeding square:

```
N A B H I
A D A I H
B A R A B
H I A D A
I H B A B
```

Square Two, Book One, Chapter One, 'To Know Future Things'

Using The Abramelin, And Other Number Or Letter Squares, In Magical Operations

MAGIC WITH WORD AND NUMBER SQUARES

The process of using number and letter squares for their specific purpose is simplicity itself. First, it is necessary to determine if the work may actually be accomplished. In other words, you have to know that it is physically possible to accomplish whatever it is that you wish to do. Building a bridge to Hawaii from San Francisco is impossible, so are a great many other far less complex tasks, some of which at first glance may look to be possible. Asking for the impossible is silly, as if you are asking for something that cannot be done, your reputation as a magician will suffer among the spirits, and other inhabitants of the non-physical world will ignore you. In this case, your reputation and abilities may collapse even before you are well started on your magical career.

Make certain that what you ask is possible, and be sure you think about this seriously. You must think of how what you desire to happen might possibly occur. If you cannot think of several ways it might happen, it is most likely an impossibility, and you should not waste time asking for it to happen.

Asking The Proper Question

When seeking information you also must know how to phrase the question you wish to have answered so that the answer will make sense to you. This is something that you also have to think about rationally. You should never just jump to conclusions over the questions you wish to ask. The process of asking the proper question is always one of the more important points in any form of divination. For example, in dealing with the future, you are always better off to ask, "What will be the result of my doing X?" Experience may have taught you that it is quite possible for you to do many things you should not even have attempted to accomplish. I have found myself in that regretful situation more times than I wish to recall.

As an example of asking a confusing question, simply asking if Mike and Lucy will marry might well produce a Yes answer because Lucy will eventually marry Howard, and Mike will marry Patricia after a few years time. Asking, 'What would be the result of Lucy and I marrying,' might give you the rather discouraging answer, "Divorce, or misery" as easily as "Bliss and Joy." Thus armed with the knowledge of what the result will be, you can make your choice in the matter.

Do not expect long-winded answers from spirits. If you get a word or two you will have to interpret it as best you can. You should prepare for short succinct answers, and consider that when you are phrasing your question. Asking a question that requires a long-winded answer is usually a waste of time.

The answer to a question such as, "When will Lucy and I make love," is easily misinterpreted. The specific question, "When will I take Lucy's virginity," is also not sufficiently specific to gain the answer you seek, as the lovely maiden you adore may not, in fact, be a virgin. If you ask instead, "When will I have satisfactory vaginal sex with Lucy," you must bear in mind that the answer may be never, because the sex will possibly be unsatisfactory. Asking, "When will I have vaginal sexual intercourse with Lucy," is more likely to produce a useful answer.

It is vitally important that you phrase the question properly, as you will ultimately have only one chance to ask it. Repetitively asking the same question is the fastest way to discourage and chase away a spirit that is sincerely trying to fulfill its god given function by truthfully answering your honest questions.

The next consideration is whether the question you are asking is actually worth asking. It is far easier to research the date of Waterloo in a book than it is to ask a spirit. Idle or silly questions will soon bore any spirit to tears, and cause them to depart from your presence. Then you have lost the value of the square you have been working with.

The final consideration is whether the spirit can actually accomplish the task you have set for it, in this case providing you a useful answer to your question. If you ask for the chemical composition of the atmosphere of Venus, you may well receive an answer, but it is quite likely you will not understand it. Your frames of reference, earthly symbols, and understanding of chemistry, and that of the spirit are certainly going to be very different. As a result, their answers to questions of this kind may be far different than what you desire to hear. This is one obstacle. Another obstacle is that the information you seek may actually be unavailable to the spirit, to you, or to anyone else. Some information is impossible to obtain, especially those things that are actually divine secrets.

You must always carefully think through any questions you may wish to ask, and you should take the time to gain some understanding of the possible answers you may receive. This must be done before you begin asking any questions of the spirit at all.

Phrasing questions is an art in itself, and it requires that you already know at least a little something of the answer, or possibly something of what the answer you will receive might be.

As far as the process of asking these questions are concerned, first, the squares you desire to make use of are clearly written out. They should be carefully inscribed on white paper, although I see no difficulty at all in printing them on a computer printer.

The square to be used is placed on a flat surface, the writing up, and the spirit of the square is summoned and asked the specific question the magician wishes to have answered. I have always liked the phrase, "I summon, stir, and call thee up." It seems to me to represent the epitome of summoning, as it quite literally says it all. Naturally, you may use that or whatever other summoning phrases you desire.

In the case of the two squares given above, the answer to the question appears in the mind, as an appropriate offering is made to the spirit of the square.

MISCELLANY

During the initial summoning of the spirit of the square, it is possible to ask what offering is desired for answering the question. A candle or possible two or three candles are usually sufficient, although a glass of water, wine, or some other alcoholic beverage may also be requested by the spirit. The offering is best placed in the middle of the square being used, along with a statement that it is for the spirit attached to that square.

I will add here that the spirits of the letter and number squares of Abramelin do not seem to have been used very often, despite the great reputation the book of Abramelin has for performing fearful and powerful fetes of magic. I wish you well in working with them.

16

FINDING THE NAME OF YOUR GUARDIAN ANGEL

If you have been saying the Monday prayer to your Guardian Angel for a few months, it is now time for you to expand this into learning the name of the angel assigned to assist you in life. The process for learning the name of your Guardian Angel is simple, and one that anyone can accomplish.

Before you fall asleep tonight, just say, 'Guardian Angel, I know that you are with me all of the time, but I don't know your name. Please let me know your name, so I can use it when I pray for you.'

That is a simple request for you to make. When you awaken in the morning you will find that the name of your Guardian Angel will be in prominent your mind when you awaken. Write the name down, and use it when you make your Monday prayer, thanking your Guardian Angel for his constant loving care, kindness, and guidance.

Hundreds of people have learned the names of their Guardian Angels in this way. You can as well.

Once you have learned the name of your Guardian Angel you can address them by name when you light a candle to them

on Monday mornings. You can then begin to form a close relationship with them.

The Monday Prayer To The Guardian Angel

"You who are with me in this life as my guide and protector,
I offer you this candle, which I light for you in thanksgiving, for
your constant loving care and guidance.

This prayer should be made on Monday morning before you
go to work. The continual use of the prayer has had beneficial
effects for many people.

17

SOME MAGICAL DEFINITIONS

Amulet

An amulet is a material object that is either believed to have a specific power or ability, or is believed to enhance the natural power or ability of the person who carries it. It may have religious or other connotations in the mind of the person wearing it, or in the minds of those seeing it when it is openly displayed. It may or may not have been charmed or had a spell cast on it by a magical act.

Examples of Amulets are: Religious medals, such as the Mary medal, the St. Christopher medal, the Scapular medal, the cross, or crucifix. A priest may bless all of these religious medals, if the person owning them desires for him to do so. The Star of David is a popular medal worn by Jews, as is the hand of Fatima is with Moslems. Their external physical shape easily identifies most of these religious amulets.

Other well known amulets include the rabbits foot, so called birthstones, copper bracelets supposedly worn for the relief of arthritis pain, scarabs, four leaf clovers, lucky coins, hair rings, or hair worn in a locket, charm bracelets, the cornu (horn), cones or seeds from plants or trees, Himmelbriefs or heaven letters, and many other objects.

A Talisman is very much the same as an amulet, although some people attempt to differentiate between them. In the Middle Ages, when it was believed Jews were connected to a source of magical power, because they were the only literate people in a European world of the deliberately illiterate, many Jews would write out or prepare magical charms for people, usually for a fee. As orthodox Jews wear a tallis, the charm was something made by a 'talisman,' or a man who wore a tallis. Now this is very much myth or folklore, but I happen to like it as an explanation of the name, as I know of no other.

Charm

A charm is something that is used to 'Place a Charm,' on something. The word means 'to sing,' and while charms may be written, sung, spoken, or otherwise produced, the object that is charmed may then be referred to as an amulet or talisman, or even misidentified as a charm.

The 'charm,' is actually the act of 'charming,' the object, whatever it may be. Therefore, making a charm, or charming something, is very much the same thing as casting a spell upon something, whether 'charming,' a person, place, or thing.

Spell

A spell may be spoken, sung, written, or acted out dramatically – as in a ceremonial magical act, or even as in a play, - such as the plays illustrating points of morality, as used in the higher degrees of freemasonry. Casting a spell may involve the use of a variety of incantations and or symbols, depending upon the magician and the result desired from the spell. Casting a spell is making, forming, or producing, a magical act of some kind. As an example, casting a spell may be using a particular procedure, and applying proper symbolism to enhance the willed intent of the person that is casting the spell.

SOME MAGICAL DEFINITIONS

There is no real difference between charming something and casting a spell on something, although curators, healers, and others often refer to their healing acts as charming, especially when using spoken words to stop blood, remove warts, or to heal various illnesses. Thus, charming is often used to refer to using magic to heal, while casting a spell on something is more frequently used to refer to applying magic for purely material aims, usually for obtaining something.

Just as anything material, any person, place, or thing, may be charmed or have spell cast on it, there is no limit to the variety of magical acts that may be performed to this end. They depend only on the desires, symbolism, and intent of the magician who is performing the magical act.

Taboo

The word Taboo is derived from the Polynesian word Tabu, indicating a prohibition placed on something for some reason. Typical Taboos are those involving going into sacred places, eating prohibited foods forbidden either to an individual, or to a group of people, or someone performing actions that are not allowed them.

Although some religions have numerous general taboos, applying to all members of the religion, other religions have few or no taboos, either general or specific. As an example, Jews, Muslims, and many pagans do not eat pork, so pork and pork products are considered taboo to them. Some religions, such as Judaism, prohibit men and women from having sexual intercourse when the woman is menstruating. Incest, sexual contact between a father and daughter, a brother and sister, or mother and son, is a common social taboo that is currently found in our own society.

The peer pressure of social convention enforce all taboos. Often there are myths concerning the terrible fates of those who have broken the taboo, adding to the weight of tradition. Few taboos have any physical reality in the real world, including the various social taboos our modern society holds so dear. Non-the less, the enforcement of social taboos is often backed by the might of both the civil and criminal law. For example, marriages that might be considered incestuous are forbidden in all states of the United States with each state defining just what they consider to be an incestuous marriage in their domain. It should be unnecessary to state that the various definitions of incest are not all identical.

The same is true for those many laws concerning the age of consent, which are also a social taboo. Although the Virgin Mary was said to have born Christ when she was only thirteen years old, most of the states of the United States hold that the age of consent should be eighteen, making the Christian God, who impregnated the Virgin Mary, a pedophile in the United States, and most of the rest of the world.

A few religions apply taboos specifically to people when they are made members of the religion. An example would be giving the initiate into the Santeria or Voudon religious practice certain behavior or dietary taboos, specific to them. Usually they would receive these taboos upon their initiation into the religion. In some cases, the house, or 'temple,' (Homfort) may have specific and unique taboos that apply to all of its members, but do not necessarily apply to members of the same religion attached to another 'temple,' or house.

Superstition

We might state that Taboos are Superstitions; as for the most part they are socially accepted beliefs that have no real basis in the physical world. However, most people who hold to social taboos do so with a tenacity of belief that is unreal. They can view superstitions as beliefs that may or may not be held by people, but are considered to be generally false. However, to these same people, Taboos have an aura of almost divine permanency. Thus superstitions may be questioned and explained, but taboos are usually accepted as permanent statements of a fact.

A superstition is literally a transcendent belief, thus a belief that takes precedence over other beliefs. The number of human superstitions is legend, and well beyond counting, although several dictionaries and encyclopedias of superstitions have been published explaining many of them. Most of these superstitions are either culturally or socially located, and thus either have little power, or are unknown in the wider world.

Some superstitions are modern, such as 'Step on a crack and break your mother's back,' something that was unknown until people began living in cities that had paved sidewalks, in the mid to late 1800's. Most children growing up in the in the rural countryside at that time had never heard of it.

A few superstitions have a basis in some real event in the past; such as the ill fortune those of European descent commonly associate with Friday The Thirteenth. This day supposedly gained its evil reputation because the King of France, Philip the Good, seized what he could of the personnel, buildings, and property of the Order Of Knights Templar on a Friday the thirteenth in 1307.

The seizure of the Knights Templars property, of which the king got far less than he had expected to receive, ended both the Knights Templars, and the practice of international commercial banking in Europe for several hundred years. This brought about an economic collapse all over Europe within something less than a decade. That time of economic depression lasted for well over a century, setting back the economic recovery of Europe from the dark ages by another three hundred years, as the depression was barely softening before the black plague hit the European continent in 1448. The result of the seizure of the Templars was an unfortunate event indeed, although the once powerful King of France, Philip the Good, did not live to see the disaster he had begun fully unfold to embrace Europe.

Magic

Magic is the application of human knowledge to the laws of the natural universe in order to bring about some desired effect through the application of symbolism, and the willed intent of the magician. Being able to perform what are generally referred to as acts of magic is one stage in the gradual spiritual development of a human being. Becoming a magician is not the end stage of spiritual development, and is often only an unwanted distraction to the person who is sincerely trying to come close to their creator.

However, the ability to practice magic seems to be a stage that all those who aspire to develop themselves spiritually must pass through. While some are caught by the glamour of that stage, others seem to have no difficulty at all ignoring their development of so called magical powers, and moving on in their real quest, toward coming closer to their creator.

False Religions

It should be obvious to the observant person that all religions are false on their face, as none of them can actually deliver anything of what they promise. Their efforts are based on programming and brainwashing their adherents, so they can only think along the lines desired, and within the bounds set, by the religious authorities.

As a result, these false religions storm and speak valiantly against anyone, and especially any institution, that can actually 'deliver the goods.' An example of this is found among the Fundamentalist Christians, who rarely if ever are able to heal anyone through prayer, but who constantly vigorously oppose those who heal through charming or other magical practices. The fact that Christ practiced magic, and said that successful magic could not be either evil or satanic (When he said, "A house divided against itself cannot stand.") is overlooked in the fury of these lost souls to condemn those people who practice magic for any purpose.

All of the major religions condemn the practice of magic, because they cannot perform it, and have no idea how to learn how to do it, as having a fanatic belief in anything is a solid bar, and a total mental prohibition, to true spiritual development. Through calling others satanic, these fanatic religions have themselves become the living embodiments of evil on the earth. They have turned away from the words of the bible they claim to hold sacred and have become repositories of the current socially approved, and very edited version of their religion, which actually often has little or nothing to do with what either Christ or St Paul actually preached.

As an example, where in the Bible does it say that you should hold church on Sunday, the first day of the week? Where in the Bible does Christ directly condemn either polygamy or slavery? None of these ideas are even mentioned in the Bible by either Christ or St Paul.

These advocates of socially approved falsity and destructive mental programming surely will receive their just reward when to their great surprise they perish in spirit after their physical death.

Fortune Telling Or Divination

The process of divination is supposedly to learn the will of the divine. In fact, it is a method of learning the most probable of the many probable outcomes of a specific situation or of the matter being considered. The quality of the divination depends entirely on the clarity with which the querant poses the question, and the clarity of the diviner to present an answer.

Most methods of fortune telling or divination have a 'prop,' as well as a means of study of the system involved. Astrology uses the horoscope, card readers use either playing cards or Tarot cards, while some fortune tellers use runes, others palmistry, numerology, and so forth. Few readers use crystal balls today, but some do, while an even smaller number use the magic mirror. In all cases, the validity of the reading depends on the skill of the reader more than on the system or prop they may use.

A few readers give legitimate cold readings, which is usually a matter of reading the sub conscious mind of the querent, and giving the querent the information consciously. Because there are a few readers who can actually do this, there are a large number of false 'cold readers,' some of whom use props of various kinds, such as Tarot Cards, Palmistry, or even crystal balls. These false cold readers recite a memorized 'patter,' to their unsuspecting subjects. Many psychologists have memorized something of this kind of 'patter,' and feed it to their clients in their therapy sessions as if it were a revelation of some kind.

> 'I see (or believe) that you have some major unresolved issues with your father (or mother), so you (we) had best attempt to work them out in our sessions before you go any further with your life. Please write out what you believe to be the five most important of these issues are, and bring the list to our next therapy session, where we will begin discussing them and ridding you of them permanently.'

These cold readings, whether pretended diviners, gypsies, psychotherapists, or others give them, are always fraudulent, and should be considered so. This kind of patter can usually be recognized by the fluidity with which the person speaks them, as if they are a well-rehearsed part of their reading practice.

Real readers usually have to pause between sentences or paragraphs and consult their props, to gain more information. This means their information is not forthcoming in a steady stream, nor is it released tortuously from inside of them, as is found in some false medium's efforts to 'sound authentic,' by straining their voice and pretending that speaking in trance is difficult. Well-trained mediums, such as religious mediums, speak in either a normal voice, or in the voice of their deity. But they speak without any strain or hesitation in their voice.

Mediums, and Channelers

In the mid 1970's and 80's there was a flood of books supposedly 'channeled from the higher planes,' concerning a variety of spiritual topics. Like many of the similar books written in the 1880's and 90's by many other supposedly 'spiritual,' people, these books all advocated what was a currently socially acceptable form of spiritual development, although one that usually did not involve going to the established church every Sunday.

In fact, most real forms of spiritual development have nothing at all to do with what people consider to be socially acceptable spiritual actions. Most spiritual teachers throughout the world urge their students to participate in social attendance at community religious events, although few find it necessary to do so in the more secular parts of Europe or America.

As but one example of true spiritual teaching, a not very well known but very valid spiritual teacher in Manhattan, New York City teaches his students only through the use of jokes and funny stories. Several of his students have become quite illuminated through his teaching. Compare that approach with the dour faced clerics who speak only of sin and damnation in the after life to their cowed congregations.

Another true spiritual teacher is quite famous for telling his students to cease praying until they can actually pray. A third, who wished to write books to assist in the process of human evolution, was forced to start his own publishing company to avoid having his books edited to death by people who knew nothing of the subject and were uninterested in pursuing it.

Many years ago, I was told that living people had to have living spiritual teachers, while spirits have to have spirits as spiritual teachers. Having witnessed a couple of spirit teachers in action, I am in complete agreement with this idea. Neither of the 'Spirit Teachers,' liked hearing this when I mentioned it to them.

There are a few religious mediums that are very worthwhile and quite sincere. These mediums do not give private readings, and they do not advertise. However, they are found in every major city in the country, doing what they are supposed to do for people. Sometimes this involves healing; some times it involves giving people practical advice. These mediums do not write books or channel spirit guides either.

Clairvoyants, Psychics, and Psychometricians

Having any of these abilities, if they are real, is not a 'gift.' These abilities are always a burden for the person who has them. Unless the individual is able to conceal themselves from other people at an early age, they will be treated like a freak, an odd ball, or even as a monster, by the world. This makes it very hard, if not almost impossible for the child to have a normal life when they are growing up.

The first thing the psychic child has to learn is to not discuss what they see, as most parents are quite unsympathetic to their children saying anything that is not wholly conventional. Telling people things about their life they may not want to hear will usually bring severe physical punishment upon the child who speaks up. This will destroy their psychic abilities permanently. I have personally witnessed several such distressingly embarrassing incidents. It is the ignorance of the parent that is at fault in these instances.

The occurrence of physical punishment for speaking is especially true if the child warns someone of something that involves either antisocial or unconventional behavior. "Hi daddy, Mommie was playing with uncle George today, they both went to the bedroom for a long time." This is a statement that will cause trouble if the child physically witnessed it, but if it were given from a psychic perspective, the result would usually be much worse. It should not take much reflection to understand this difficulty could become a real burden for the child to bear.

A child reporting on things that are going to happen will often be blamed, quite irrationally, for causing them. This is particularly true in the event of predicting great emotional upsets scheduled to occur in the future, such as fires, the death of a person or a pet, and so forth. This is the shoot the messenger syndrome, and unfortunately it is a common response people have to hearing such things.

Naturally the same is true of the telepathic child, but the child who is telepathic from birth usually will learn to be silent before they are old enough to begin speaking. The psychic child is not usually telepathic, so they often blurt out things that would much better be left unsaid.

Clairvoyance often includes the ability to see things at a distance currently referred to as remote viewing. However, it also usually includes being able to see into the immediate future.

SOME MAGICAL DEFINITIONS

Without training, psychic children and clairvoyants can become stunted or forced to abandon their ability completely. In this case, these abilities become 'wild talents,' often popping up in disruptive ways later on in the person's life.

Psychometricians are those sometimes referred to as spoon benders. They have a degree of psychic control over physical objects. The depth and nature of their control is not constant between different people, but varies widely. Some can only work with fine electronic circuits, such as healing damaged microchips; others can bend spoons, while a very few can move heavy machinery.

Fortunately for long suffering parents, Psychometery is a very rare talent. Like several other 'wild talents,' it usually does not develop in the child until the child begins going through puberty. The most common manifestation of this talent is seen in the poltergeist phenomena. This is the 'noisy ghost,' and is frequently a sign that someone in the home has the Psychometric talent, and is passing through puberty.

The problem of the poltergeist is particularly a problem in sexually repressive homes, where the cure is usually far more difficult to administer. If the source of the disturbance is a pubescent male, as is usually is, the solution is absurdly simple, get the boy to have frequent sexual contact with a willing female. In the more rare case of a female being the source of the disturbance, get her on birth control, and then get her having frequent sexual contact with a willing male. Having guilt free sexual relations at least once a week is about the minimum contact required to completely eliminate the poltergeist problem.

In addition to the usually uncontrolled ability to toss things around, those with this talent are also able to 'sense the vibes' of objects and tell something about their origin and often their ownership. This is similar to a parlor game that used to be played many years before television, in which several objects were passed around and the people holding them were to guess where they came from, or who owned them. Those people with this interesting talent are able to develop it in a positive way through playing this game; although there are also some other exercises they should practice to further develop themselves.

Palmistry

Also known as chiromancy, palmistry is a very old art, and like astrology, dates back to an origin somewhere in Asia or the ancient near east. It is another life long study, which has no fascination for those only interested in the superficial art of telling fortunes. Modern science has found there are telltale signs of several diseases that may be diagnosed in the hand long before they become noticeable as physical symptoms.

Like astrology, there are at least as many crackpots in the field of palmistry as there are those who have something worthwhile to say about it. The Egyptians believed the destiny of a person was written in the palms of their hands and the soles of their feet. Thus, they read both.

In addition to reading the hands and feet, there are also divinatory arts involving reading other parts of the physical body. Reading the face was popular about twenty years ago, when several books introduced the Chinese system of face reading. It is also possible to gain information by reading other parts of the physical body, such as the breasts and pubic hair of women. Of all of these divinatory arts, Palmistry is the one more frequently encountered.

Occultism

Although the mention of occultism raises a fearful specter to the Christian fundamentalist, it is simply the study of those things that are hidden away by society. The Greek New Testament for example is an occult text, as it is certainly not often studied outside of biblical seminaries. To occult means to hide, as in the earth occulting the moon, as it does during a lunar eclipse. The idea that something is hidden is frightening to those who have closed and tightly programmed fanatical minds. To them, nothing that tries their beliefs can possibly be worthwhile, and therefore these things are considered to be evil on their face.

The study of the occult usually refers to the study of those things normally hidden from public sight. In common usage it refers to astrology, magic, and so forth, but it could equally refer to rhetoric, elocution, and platform oratory, subjects that are now 'occult,' as they are no longer studied in the modern educational system, although once they were. The myth that studying occult subjects is damaging to the individual is a common one, although it is untrue. Studying the occult is no more damaging than studying differential calculus, something that is another rocky shore for some people.

Satanism

Satanism is a branch or a sub-set of the Christian religion. Despite the beliefs of many Christians, there is no other religion that treats the personification of human evil in the way that Christianity, especially Protestant Fundamentalist Christianity, does. Satanists like Christians base their doctrine on the Christian Bible, especially upon the New Testament.

A little background information may be required first. In Zoroastrian philosophy it was proposed that there were equal good and evil deities, and that this earth was their battlefield, in which they struggled for superiorly. People were supposed to be good, to help the good deity in his struggle with the evil deity. There was a great deal more to their theology of course, but this dualistic idea was an approach that was enthusiastically received in certain schools of philosophy, both in the Middle East and in some of the philosophic schools of Greece.

Plato opposed this idea, and so did Aristotle his student, so Alexander, the student of Aristotle, upon conquering Persia, killed all of the Zoroastrian and Magian priests he could find, and burned a great many of their books. As usually happens when someone attempts the destruction of a religion, the Zoroastrians went underground, and hid both their priests and books from Alexander. To this day, sincere orthodox Zoroastrians curse the name of Alexander The Great in their daily prayers.

That is not a valuable legacy for any man. After the invasion and conquest of Persia by the warriors of Islam, many of the remaining Zoroastrians migrated to India, where they are known today as Parsees.

With the invasion of Alexander, the ideas of the Zoroastrian religion spread once again, and this time infiltrating the lower layer of society, so the Egyptians for one began to see Set, the god or deity of the underworld as a directly evil figure. About 200 BC, many religions had this belief in a directly evil figure added to them, or the religion took one of their existing deities, and made their attributes more directly evil.

Next we must look at Satan as he is shown in the Old Testament. In the book of Job, Satan is one of the (many) sons of God, and he is designated as the tempter of humankind. Acting in a role similar to the prosecuting attorney in a trial, he is hardly directly evil, and has no power but that of offering temptation, from which the God fearing person will turn.

In the New Testament we meet a different and far more powerful Satan, one who tempts Jesus in the desert. Recall that Satan offered Jesus the kingship of all of the earth if he worshiped him. Some temptation, Eh? Satan goes on to say that the disposition of the wealth of the earth is in his hands. So according to this view, the evil Satan has won the struggle, and now he may dispose of the wealth and power of the earth as he desires.

This whole idea of the devil taking mankind from the straight and narrow to corrupt mankind became a main point of Christian theology. The church preached that the only way a human could be saved from the eternal fires of hell was to devote themselves completely to the will and desires of the church. As time went on, from about 350 to about 700 AD, this desire of the church to have everyone subordinate themselves to its will became increasingly the theme of European society. As a result, less deviance from the ideal of total obedience to religious authority was allowed to anyone.

Except those at the top of course. You don't think the perfumed people bought this nonsense do you? The rich and powerful, as well as the nobility didn't buy it, not a penny's worth.

SOME MAGICAL DEFINITIONS

They gave public praise to the church, but privately did not believe a bit of the church's theology.

So around the year 1022, when Benedict the Ninth was consecrated pope (at the age of eleven according to some), he set about doing what most of the previous popes had done, enjoying himself and generally raising hell while being outwardly theologically perfectly devout and praiseworthy as pope.

One of the more interesting things Benedict the Ninth did was to formalize the rite of the black mass, and introduce the rite of the goat of Mendes (The goat of a thousand young). He did this last by having sex with a female goat while a male goat was servicing one of his many lady friends. This stirring event happened at the main altar of St Peter's Cathedral in Rome. He also held several 'black masses,' there, and probably with the assistance of some of his more 'liberal' theologians. He formally regularized the 'Black Mass, and described the various positions of the traditional naked woman who was the altar.

To this day, although Benedict the Ninth appears three times on the list of popes (He was kicked off the papal throne three times, the last kick kept him off.) most historians of the papacy have little good to say about him. The Latin texts are far more reveling, he is called the worst of the popes, and the scourge of the papacy. In some of the Latin texts, he is called a lot worse.

Never less, because of the statement that Satan has the things of this world to offer to those who worship him, Satanism has become very popular to those who wish to gain money and power in the world. And to this day these worshipers of the principle of evil tend to follow at least an outline of the ritual format laid down almost a thousand years ago by Pope Benedict the Ninth.

Of course the most interesting point to this is that only a baptized and confirmed Christian can be a Satanist, as it is only in the Christian religion that Satan has this kind of power, and the ability to grant worldly favors to his worshipers. In the other religions that have Satan as a minor member of their theology, his works amount to almost nothing, except as his being a tempter of humankind.

In the 1960's Anton Salzar LaVey, a former circus, and bur- lesque performer founded what he called the 'Church of Satan,' in San Francisco California. This church; was based more on the self help doctrines of Dale Carnegie than on any theological information taken from the bible. LaVey wrote his own 'Satanic Bible,' which has become a popular 'standard' seller, if not a best seller among books. His organization has nothing at all to do with real religious Satanism.

Demonolaters

Demons may or may not be associated with any specific re- ligion. Christianity, Judaism, Islam, Buddhism, and several other religions have a variety of demons attached to them. So do books like the Greater and Lesser Keys of Solomon, the Book of Abramelin, and many other grimoires or texts dealing with summoning spirits and demons.

These demons, of whatever source, religious or not, are es- sentially thoughtforms that are activated and maintained by the emotions of those who believe in them. As with all thought- forms, especially strong ones, it is possible to ask the thought- forms, spirits, or demons, for assistance in one's life.

This means it is sometimes useful to work with these de- mons, or at least, ask them to do work for yourself or others. The idea of summoning spirits and entities into the magician's circle is one of the ways in which though forms, such as these so-called demons, may be worked with. There are a number of books giving the information required to summon these spirits and ask them to do a variety of things for the magician.

Demonolaters are those who work with, and often worship, demons. Some demonolaters work in groups, a few of these groups are quite similar to churches, while others practice ceremonial magic with these spirits and demons in lodges, some of them using the degrees and other paraphernalia of ceremo- nial magic or other occult lodges.

Witchcraft

Despite the variety of witches in the world today, and their many enthusiastic claims of antique origin it is a provable fact that there are no continuous lines of witchcraft dating from the Middle Ages. In fact, most of these so-called witch covens are actually groups of rather giddy nature worshipers. To believe that witches form powerful evil conspiracies is either just a form of sick humor, or an indication of the paranoia present in the believer.

18

REMOTE INFLUENCE
Persuasion At A Distance

Please use this information in harmony with the techniques explained in my book, 'Mental Influence,' published by Xlibris, and available from them, your local booksellers, or at Amazon.com . The information given below was written to supplement class information before that book was written. It is only a supplement to the information given in that book.

~-~

Remote influence is the name given to the act of one living human being mentally influencing another living human, without any physical form of communication between them. This subtle influence is usually exerted at a distance – thus, it is known as remote influence. Remote influence may also be used to influence the non-physical part of an organization, institution, business, or other non-human entity. This latter use is less well known, but it is as effective as influencing another person in this way.

As remote influence is exerted entirely through mental action, there is no limitation as to the physical location of the person being influenced. The subject of this influence could be sitting next to the person influencing them, or they could be on another continent. Furthermore, it is not even necessary for the person influencing their subject to know a great deal about the individual or entity they are influencing. A photograph, or even their name, may be sufficient to allow the influencing person to 'tune into' the person they wish to influence, and thus direct their mental influence to them.

Before you believe that this is some horrible evil form of mind control, it is necessary to understand that the depth of the influence being exerted upon the influenced entity may or may not be sufficient to make the influenced individual change their thoughts, beliefs, or behavior, in any way at all. This is because the information originating from the influencing person enters into the influenced person's sub conscious mind. The influence intended to change the entity's beliefs, thoughts, or behavior does not necessarily ever even reach their conscious mind.

Because the influenced person is not consciously aware of the influence being directed to them, this influence may not result in any discernable change in the thoughts or behavior of the subject entity at all.

The human sub conscious mind is not rational, it is emotional, but it is also the store of the individuals memories. Thus, information coming into the sub conscious mind is often just stored away and not ever reviewed, or even recognized, by the recipient's conscious mind. When any influence is presented to the subconscious mind, it remains present in the subconscious mind, but it is unlikely to be acted upon until, or unless, there is some pressing need to bring the information forward to consideration by the person's conscious mind. Unfortunately for the person wishing to influence the subject, many times this pressing need might never occur in the lifetime of the influenced individual. Thus they will not sense this information during their lifetime.

In addition to the proven natural ability of humans to mentally influence other people, it is also possible for people to mentally influence animals, plants, and even to influence a number of inanimate objects. Although this may sound surprising, these effects have actually been both reported and experienced by a great many people.

Although some people seem to have a natural talent for this work, for most others, to be able to master the ability to influence others, requires them to first train their own mind. Obviously, a trained mind has a far greater ability to influence other people, animals, and even physical objects, than an untrained mind.

The person wishing to master this art must begin by learning to concentrate their mind. Once an individual is able to sharply focus their mind, they can apply that focus to any purpose they desire. The person with a focused mind who wishes to influence others will be better able to direct their focused thoughts to the person they desire to influence. In this event, the influence will be received directly into the sub conscious mind of the person they desire to influence.

Influencing Others Is Not Unique
As We Constantly Influence Other People
Through Verbal Persuasion or Salesmanship

It has been said the ability to persuade and influence others is the key to all success. Persuasion is certainly the most prevalent form of communication between people. We all seem to be in a constant attempt to either persuade, or influence those with whom we come into contact. Please think about this for a moment, considering the way you attempt to influence other people in your daily life. For many of us, it is almost a continual activity.

Whether we are aware of it or not, all humans constantly influence other people in the course of their daily life. We accomplish this with our spoken words, and thoughts, as well as with other people's interpretations of our physical body language and our habitual mannerisms. We usually influence others consciously with our speech, but we must recognize that the words we speak also enter into the subconscious mind of the one hearing them. The person receiving our words will interpret the words they hear based on our tone of voice, the emphasis we used in speaking the words, and the thoughts we project to them as we speak. They will also sub consciously consider the way we present ourselves to them physically. Our dress and physical appearance, our mannerisms and physical actions as we speak to them, also influence both the other person's perception of us, and of what we are saying.

In addition to any influence exerted by our words, we influence other people unconsciously with our thoughts, which may be either in harmony with our words, or different from the words we are speaking. Usually the influence of our thoughts on other people is completely unconscious on our part. Once we are aware of the possibilities of exerting mental influence on other people, it may occasionally, or at least more frequently, become a willed conscious action on our part to deliberately direct our thoughts to others in an attempt to influence them.

We should also be aware that we influence other people through our mannerisms, including the way we move our physical bodies, and especially the expression on our face, as we speak. This is often referred to as our body language, but it also means our facial expression and particularly the eye and lip movements we make as we speak. Correctly or incorrectly, people often read a great deal into these visual clues.

Many people have habitual mannerisms they engage in as they speak. One example of this is the way some people bob their head as they talk, tossing them around as if their heads were a small boat on a stormy sea. There are many other similar physical mannerisms people have, all of them have significance to the trained and discerning eye. Although these mannerisms may often be distracting to those who listen to them, the people we are speaking to often read a great deal into these visual clues.

When we attempt to persuade someone with our words, we are using verbal influence. In doing this, we are usually combining conscious verbal influence with whatever sub conscious influence we are able to bring to bear to assist our verbal persuasion, or the verbal 'sales pitch' we are directing toward the listener. This is the most common example of conscious and direct mental influence I can think of. The child trying to ver-

bally explain that he did not commit a prohibited act to his dis-
believing parent typifies this type of often-strained verbal
persuasion.

Salesmanship is probably the most effective, and best-
known means of consciously directed verbal influence, or persuasion. It occurs in everyday direct person-to-person conscious communication, as at the store, conversation between
friends and co-workers, and in talking with strangers. Techniques of salesmanship used in the persuasion of others are not
limited to the monetary communications usually called to mind
when we think of salesmanship. All of us use these techniques
of verbal influence, consciously or unconsciously, every day of
our lives.

Courtroom legal pleadings, our talking with other people in
stores and at work, and even romantic seductions are all based
upon what we may call salesmanship. These are all examples
of our attempts to verbally persuade others, which, when
placed in a commercial context are usually referred to as salesmanship.

The actual ability of one person to successfully consciously
persuade or influence other people has been shown by investi-
gation to be based upon several factors. Some of the more important of these factors are:

A. - The physical appearance the speaker makes. If people look at us as having a favorable appearance, they will pay
more attention to what we say, and will remember our words
longer. If we have a good physical appearance, they will also
be more likely to believe us, and accept what we tell them as
being true. This is the reason we must always dress for the oc-
casion in which we are involved. One of the primary influences
on our dress should be our desire to make others accept us and
believe what we say.

B. - Our manner of speech. If we speak in an educated
and clear voice, without hesitation, impediments, or fear, the
people we are speaking to will pay more attention to what we
say, and will remember our words longer. They will also be

more likely to believe us and to accept what we tell them as being true.

The art of clear speaking is known as elocution, and in the early years of the twentieth century, it was a common subject of study in most elementary schools. Speaking softly in a well-modulated low-pitched tone of voice assures listeners of our higher status, and demonstrates to them our right to speak on the subject, as well as reassures those who hear us that we believe what we are saying. Loud, higher pitched, or squeaky voices grate on the ears. They often make people believe the speaker is subordinating themselves to the listeners. Such voices do not get the message across.

Most people can accept that some women normally speak in a high pitched or squeaky manner, but they will mentally degrade any man who does so. This is why those who are to represent the public must always speak in a lower toned voice to be more widely accepted by those who hear them.

C. - The words we say. Research has shown that certain words and phrases cause a statistically larger number of people to respond favorably to the speaker than do other words and phrases. The real estate industry, for example, has developed a number of positive influencing ways to talk to someone a real estate salesman is showing a house to. The real estate salesperson knows that certain phrases, applied at certain stages of the home showing process, make the average purchaser more likely to buy than other phrases. The wise salesman follows this proven 'sales script,' and avoids saying anything at all that would discourage the person from making the purchase.

D. - Our focus on the person we are attempting to persuade. We must maintain our focus on the person we are attempting to persuade and not allow ourselves to be distracted by other things. If we maintain a warm and friendly focus on the person we are speaking to, they will pay more attention to what we say, and remember our words longer. They will also be more likely to believe us and to accept what we tell them as being true.

E. - The rapport the speaker has with the other person, or with their audience. This rapport is most easily developed by those who trust their intuition, are prepared to like everyone, who appeal to the desires of those others they wish to influence, and who position themselves in a favorable way with other people.

Positioning is done by approaching other people on their level, neither to high or too low. Just as you must avoid talking down to others, you must also avoid talking up to others. Always try your best to approach other people as an equal, regardless of what you may think of them, either as individuals or as a group.

If We Wish To Convince Someone, We Must First Pay Attention To Them

Please observe the end result of any effort to persuade someone is always to have the people we are speaking with to pay attention to what we say, and remember our words for as long a time as possible. We want the people we are speaking with to believe us, accepting what we tell them as being true. Therefore, if we are to be good persuaders, we must make use of all possible techniques we can master to gain the results we desire.

This is the best reason in the world for learning to focus our attention on others, and pay close attention to them when they speak. By paying close attention to someone, you are honoring them and convincing them you believe in their worth as a human being. This will also convince them to pay close attention to you, when you speak to them.

In a way, we are all salesmen. We do our best to persuade other people every day. We all want certain things out of life, both tangible and intangible. To obtain the things we want we must persuade other people to give them to us. This is the motive for our learning to use the art of persuasion properly;

whether we use persuasion for applying either direct or remote influence to the person we are working with.

Remote influence is simply working to persuade people remotely to do what we wish them to do, instead of trying to persuade them in person. We may use remote influence to persuade other people to give us what we want, or to act as we desire. When we use persuasion, we are always trying to convince or sway others, whether the person we are attempting to persuade is physically present or not. In the case of remote influence, we are doing this mentally, and usually from a distance.

We have all used remote influence unconsciously in the past, as when we wishfully dream of our desires for someone, or talk about someone. In this case, we are sub consciously attempting to influence their sub conscious mind. It would certainly be a good idea for us to learn to use remote influence both consciously and deliberately. Once we master the ability to consciously and deliberately apply both verbal persuasion and remote influence to others, we will find our life will quickly become considerably easier.

The Mental Atmosphere

We may or may not be aware that we generate our own mental atmosphere. However, when we ponder, or seriously consider something mentally, we are thinking in our own mind, but we are also radiating and transmitting our thoughts and emotions into the non-physical 'atmosphere' surrounding us. We do this even though these thoughts and emotions may not be specifically directed at another person. You may have noticed that under such circumstances a person may have generated a particular mental atmosphere around themselves. In the case of pondering, troubling, or deeply serious thought, our thoughts may have generated a heavy, serious, and possibly even a stodgy, or depressing, mental atmosphere around us.

The mental atmosphere with which we surround ourselves is but one example of the way human beings unconsciously project their thoughts and emotions. If you attempt to try and sense the 'mental atmosphere' of those whom you contact in your daily life, you will soon find that by doing so you can gain some insights into the person themselves.

As an example, the mental atmosphere around children playing is often light and happy, as they radiate joy and happiness at their play. The contrast between the atmosphere surrounding playing children and ponderous thinkers are two rather extreme examples of people's mental influence extending out around them and forming a particular kind of non-physical 'mental atmosphere.' Learning to sense the mental atmosphere surrounding other people is a valuable trait. Being very mentally and emotionally still, or remaining mentally calm and peaceful within yourself, will aid you in developing this sense. That will open you to sensing just what the other person is radiating with their thoughts and emotions.

To successfully influence other people your own mental atmosphere must initially be rather bland and unemotional, possibly even somewhat boring. Once you begin to interact with them, your mental atmosphere should change to one of enthusiastic attention directed toward the other person. You should not be concerned with anything other than the person who is object of your influence.

When you are attempting to influence or persuade others, you should not be in any strong emotional state yourself. While it is sometimes possible to influence another person mentally when the influencer is in a strong emotional state, it is not a good idea, as the control required to effectively do so is usually entirely absent. This means our ability to influence another person is considerably lessened.

The best mental atmosphere to have is one of slight curiosity, such as you would have when meeting a new person you believe you might wish to have as a friend. Holding this bland but slightly curious mental and emotional state firmly in your mind usually gives the best results, both in meeting and influencing other people.

Defining Remote Influence

REMOTE INFLUENCE

We must limit our definition of remote influence to those influences that are entirely non-physical, and that may or may not involve the influencing person being located near the person who is being influenced. We must also accept that any immediate response to the remote influence of another person is not a normal characteristic of remote influence.

Because people are usually looking for the attention, approval, and validation of others, the vast majority of humans are usually quite open to being influenced or persuaded by other people. This leads people to be as open to being remotely influenced as it does to their being influenced by something someone says to them, or by a commercial advertisement, they may either see or hear.

The majority of people are wide open to the influence of others, whether this influence originates from ordinary conversation, conscious persuasion, deliberate salesmanship, or from conscious and deliberately planned remote influence. However, just because a person is open to being influenced, this does not mean the person will act, either immediately or over time, on any influence they may receive.

How many automobile advertisements do you see in the course of a day? How many automobiles do you purchase? Obviously you will not act on most of the influences that are directed toward you each day, whether this influence is in the form of commercial advertisements, conversation, or remote influence.

A far smaller number of people are not easy to either persuade or influence, either in person or indirectly. These people are occasionally aware that someone may be attempting to influence them, either consciously or sub consciously, but they will usually do nothing about it, as the influence being sent them, being consciously ignored, or neglected by them, will simply die off. The energy of any influence, whether remote or in person, will usually dissipate in a short time if the energy of the thought being sent to the person is not matched by some conscious interest, or some subconscious thoughts found within the mind of the person themselves.

This is the primary reason successful remote influence must always be applied repetitively. A single application of remote influence is only very rarely productive of any results. On the other hand, the continuous repetition of a single theme in remote influence is usually quite effective. Naturally, it is far more effective if the theme strikes some chord within the mind of person being influenced. Even if it does not strike a chord within the person, repetition of the same influence tends to build a base, so that should the person accept some similar idea in the future, it will find a ready prepared seedbed to allow the newly accepted idea to successfully germinate.

There has been some scientific research done on the general subject of remote influence. Most of the scientific research confirms the statements made above. Dr. William Brand Ph.D. has written, 'Distant Mental Influence,' about remote influence, in which much of this scientific research is mentioned. He also mentions the flexibility of time, stating that people can look both forward and backward in time by using this natural human ability. Dr. Brand believes that with only minimal training, anyone can learn to use these mental skills for their own benefit.

In the late nineteenth century, Dr. Julien Ochotowicz investigated claims of remote mental influence made by distant healers, and found them valid. After some study of the subject he was inspired to write a book of his investigations, which was published in Europe as, 'The Mental Suggestion,' and in the United States as, 'Mental Dominance, Classics of Magnetism and Hypnotism.' Another book on the subject, written in 1908 by William Walker Atkinson, is called 'Practical Mental Influence,' while a third book by Draja Mickaharic is, 'Mental Influence.' Most of these books are available from both local and on line booksellers, such as Amazon, or Barnes and Noble.

Self-Training for Remote Influence

Aside from learning to concentrate and focus the mind, freeing it from all distractions, it is also necessary that the individual who wishes to mentally influence others learn how to create a mental image of the one they wish to influence. In some cases they should create an image of exactly what action they desire the influenced person to take. This is called visualization, and may be either done from memory, or by using a photograph as an aid. These two abilities, mental concentration and visualization, are the two most important abilities required for success in any field of magic. It is not at all surprising that they are both needed to successfully practice the art of remote mental influence.

It is usually helpful if the person trying to influence another is able to visualize an image of exactly what action they desire the influenced person to take. The ability of emotional control is also required for success in influencing others. As one example, you may desire to have the person you are influencing as a lover, but you should not become emotionally involved with them until they have expressed strong emotional involvement with you. You must not confuse your mentally influencing another person with your emotions in the matter. If you allow your emotions to run wild, your subconscious mind will be so focused on that, there will be little effort left to project the influence you desire to the person you wish to sway.

I stress again, that aside from learning to concentrate the mind, freeing it from all distractions, it is also necessary that the individual who wishes to mentally influence others learn how to create a mental image of the one they wish to influence. There are a number of well-known exercises available for developing these abilities. Which exercise you chose to use is unimportant. The important thing is that you actually take the time to work and develop these abilities if you sincerely wish to be able to remotely influence other people.

An Example Of Using Remote Influence
Do You Wish To Bring Some Desired Condition To Yourself?

If this is your desire, you should concentrate upon an image of the desired condition, knowing in your heart there is no reason why it should not appear, exactly as you desire it to come to you. As you concentrate on the picture of the imagined condition in your mind, the very effect you are looking for will gradually occur, as you are actually mentally calling that condition to yourself.

MISCELLANY

Of course, if you do not believe you deserve this positive condition, or should you believe that something, such as a defect of character, prohibits you from attaining the condition you otherwise believe you desire, that difficulty or defect must be removed before the condition may be made manifest in your life. Therefore, before you begin to attempt to call any desired condition to yourself, you should first take some time to honestly talk to yourself and decide that you are a worthy recipient of the condition you desire, and are both willing and eager to actually have it appear in your life.

Discovering The Influences That Are Bearing Upon Your Mind

If you think about the nature of the influences upon your mind, and recognize that these influences come not only from other people, but also from various forms of advertising, as well as commercial and individual puffery, such as various attempts at salesmanship, you will understand why I say that as humans, we constantly attempt to influence each other. It is impossible to evade or turn away from the many influences that come upon every human being each day of their life. Instead of trying to avoid these many influences, it becomes necessary for us to consciously make note of the influences around us, and then consciously and deliberately turn away from those influences we do not wish to be held over us. We actually have a choice as to how we are being influenced. We should take advantage of this ability to choose what influences our life.

The influences applied to us may be either positive or negative, debilitating or life enhancing. It is up to us to decide what any particular influence or attempted influence upon us actually is worth to us in our daily lives. As but one example, the increase in advertising concerning the medical treatments for various diseases has gradually increased the number of people that are being afflicted with such diseases. This increase is because such advertisements for drugs and remedies to treat diseases actually 'sell' these diseases to unwary and receptive people.

For the same reason, the number of situation comedies and dramatic television programs featuring hospitals has actually acted to promote the closing of some hospitals, as many people no longer believe those who work in hospitals have any real concerns other than their traumatic, dysfunctional, and disarrayed personal lives, they see displayed by the actors on the television screen. Thus, many of these dissuaded people try not to go to hospitals unless it becomes absolutely necessary for them to do so. Other people, influenced by these television dramas, will now go out of their way to avoid going to a hospitals at all costs.

A Self Examination Before
Beginning To Influence Another Person
Or Draw Some Physical Object To Yourself

Let us put this idea into practical terms, and relate this process to the kind of conditions you might wish to draw to yourself. Before proceeding any further, you must objectively investigate the true opportunity you have to actually influence the course of events in the manner you desire. It should be obvious that not everything in the universe is equally easy to influence. This is especially true when you initially begin working with this process. Therefore it is important you first select something that is reasonably easy for you to influence. You are looking for an effect you believe you will be able to see in the person or situation you are attempting to influence.

As one example: If you desire to win a huge amount of money in a lottery, you must realize your desires are matched by literally thousand of other people, quite probably by everyone who purchases a lottery ticket. These strong desires may not cancel each other out, but they will certainly have an ameliorating effect on each other. Thus, the power of human desire, being reduced by this strong amelioration effect, the lottery is going to be far less influenced by the desires of the players than any of those players might wish it to be.

At the same time, should you have some particular personal goal in mind, it is quite likely you will be able to draw it to yourself. The distinction here is that those goals that are more universally sought, such as winning a lottery, are always far more difficult of achievement. Therefore, before you begin working toward any goal you should take some time and see just what the nature of the goal you desire to achieve actually is.

Are your chances of achieving that goal without using non-physical influence reasonably good, or are they even possible? Assuming the goal you seek is at least possible for you to achieve, it is very likely your actually attaining it will be further enhanced by the use of remote influence. In the event it is going to be impossible or nearly impossible for you to attain that goal without using influence of some kind, it is highly unlikely that the application of any form of non-physical influence will be of real assistance to you in reaching your desired goal. Again, this will be especially true during the beginning of your efforts in mastering remote influence.

For most people, using remote influence will only enhance the opportunities presently available to them. However, if an opportunity is possible for you, using remote influence can frequently be of aid in manifesting the opportunity into physical reality. You must know what you are asking for, know that you can receive it, and work accordingly.

To use another example, if it is your desire to marry the current toast of the Hollywood screen, unless you already know her reasonably well, you will find it will be particularly difficult for you to do so. In this case, remote influence is unlikely to be of any help. Think of how many others are seeking the same goal, directly or by using whatever arts they may know, magical or otherwise.

However, if it is only your desire to get married, that is something you may rather easily accomplish, whether you are using remote influence or not. The more limited your desire, the more realistically it may actually be achieved. Be practical about this. Remote influence will not grant you the dictatorial power to rule the world. You are only trying to gain the ability to exert some hidden influence on other people. This is real magic, not the magic of TV or the movies.

The process of gaining your attainable desire is actually rather simple. First, exactly and precisely decide what you want, without putting any limit upon it. As an example, it is far easier to marry an unspecified blond woman who is physically attractive, and who likes to cook than it is to attract to yourself and marry someone who is well known by name for either her beauty or her cooking skill.

Begin your quest, for marriage or for anything else, by writing out your requirements, knowing that you need to list them in the order of their importance to you. Then look through these requirements and think about them for a day or two, rearranging them to be certain they are in the order of importance to you. Avoid putting a name or a face on the image you are developing in your mind, but now begin to visualize this person or item you have specified. You want to form the image of the person or item you desire clearly in your mind, based only on the requirements you have listed. Imagine yourself receiving your desire or meeting the person. In the event of your looking for a lover or marriage partner, see yourself talking to them, and interacting socially with this faceless unknown. The more strongly you visualize receiving your desired item, or potential lover, using one or two sessions of about ten or fifteen minutes each day, the closer you will be to drawing this item or person toward yourself.

You should also feel the joy and happiness that will be yours when you receive this person or item into your life. Think of how you will enjoy the person or item, how you will be pleased on receiving it and having it in your life. In this case, it does not matter if it is a wife or a motorcycle you desire. You must fell the joy and happiness you expect to have when what you desire appears.

When you locate the desired item, or meet someone that matches many or most of the important characteristics you have visualized, you must go out of your way to specifically draw the item or person toward you, while asking yourself if this is really the item or the person you desire. If it seems that what had presented it self to you is what you truly desire, you have found what you have been seeking.

Please bear in mind that finding a perfect match to all of the many detailed requirements on your list is highly unlikely. You must also realize that that the more requirements you make, and the more detailed these requirements are, the more limited will be your field, and the more difficult it will be for the universe to fill your request. Three or four of your major requirements are usually all you can reasonably expect to have filled when you are seeking to either find the ideal mate for yourself, draw someone to yourself, or find a desired item of some kind. Once again, you must always be both realistic and practical when attempting to influence someone, whether you are doing it in person, or through using remote influence.

A Checklist
Before Influencing Another Person

Who or what do you wish to influence?
People In General Or One Person Specifically?
An Institution, Organization, or a Business?

What Is Your Message?

Write it out in no more than twenty words.
If you wish to influence a person, appeal directly
to the person's senses, dealing with things
'seen, felt, tasted, smelled, and heard'

Realize your target will only receive general impressions, so you must use frequent repetition to reinforce your influence on your subject.

Bear in mind that Practice Makes Perfect.
To Succeed, You Must Keep At It!

Another Example Of Mental Influence
Do You Wish To Bring Some Material Object To Yourself?

In this case, knowing what the object desired is, and assuming that it is not noted for its rarity, you have only to visualize your possessing it and feel the emotion of the pleasure you feel in possessing the object. That will often be enough to begin to call the object to you. How the object you desire arrives to you must never be a consideration in this matter. Once you have firmly set yourself on visualizing the object you wish to possess, and are looking forward to enjoying your possession of the object you desire, the object will slowly begin to make its way toward you.

Because they are not particularly rare, I have often thought the best thing to begin to visualize is either coins or paper money. Visualizing a twenty-dollar bill every morning for fifteen minutes, and feeling the joy you will have putting it in your pocket will, after a time, often call the money to your hand during the course of the day. Naturally, if what you obtain is less than a twenty, you should still be both satisfied, and grateful to the universe for whatever funds you may have received. If you wish, calling money of no particular denomination to you is as effective an exercise as visualizing a twenty-dollar bill. Often it is a more fruitful exercise.

Developing Your Visualization Ability

The ability to visualize things is developed first by developing the ability to recall experiences, which is also a way of developing your memory. Remember scenes from your past, and then draw or sketch them from memory. You can also look at an illustration one day, then recall and draw it from memory the next. No great artistic talent is required for this project as it is more a matter of putting on paper the elements of the scene than it is in getting every detail perfect. Always begin with the simple and then gradually move on to sketching the more complex. Making very rough sketches is perfectly acceptable for this memory work.

Should you not like the idea of using graphic art, you can take these same scenes and write out descriptions of them. Attempt to put such detail in the scenes you write about that any person reading the description could pick it out from a number of others. Describing in words the scenes you find in pictures, even those scenes you find on picture postal cards, may be the key to learning to master this project. Later on, as you improve your work, you may well wish to make the literary description of the scene so clear that readers can imagine they are standing in the scene, experiencing it as if they lived it.

MISCELLANY

You can also recall experiences from your past in this way, sketching them or writing them out in detail. You may then visualize yourself reliving these experiences. After practicing these exercises for a few weeks, you should have expanded your ability to recall your memories, as well as increased your ability to visualize whatever scenes you wish to see.

The exercise of recalling your personal memories in detail is an excellent one, as it trains people to recall their memories, as well as to visualize those memories in full. Heading several sheets of paper with years is one way to begin this effort. Then recall what happed to you during each of those years. Begin with the more memorable events in your life, such as graduating from elementary or high school, college etc. Then gradually fill in the details naming the persons that you knew, and the situations you lived through. As you do this, the floodgates of memory will soon open and you will be able to recall almost all of the experiences of your life.

Through this process of recalling memories, it is sometimes possible to psychically straighten out someone who may have had difficulties with their life. Naturally, there is often more involved in this than has been mentioned here, but this process is often a good start to solving any psychological problems you may believe you might have.

Once you have been able to recall several of your memories in great detail, you may be ready to go into a more detailed process of visualization. Take a relatively common object, a lead pencil for example. Hold it in your hands and mentally study it as if you were going to write a very detailed report concerning its appearance. Observe the object from all sides, so that you take note of all of its possible blemishes and imperfections, as these marks are what distinguish the object you have chosen from others of its kind.

Now set the item you have selected aside, and call its memory to your mind. See the object in your 'mind's eye,' exactly as you saw it when you held it in your hands. Observe its color, shape, and the details of its surface. Practice this until you can perfectly recall each and every detail of the object you have selected, picturing it perfectly in your mind, and holding that image for several minutes. Then you should continue with other small objects, learning to recall them in all of their many tiny details. When you have mastered this exercise with three or four physical objects, you are well on your way to having mastered the art of visualization. You will find you ability to recall the look of objects and people from your memory has increased.

Manifesting Material Things

To call any material object to yourself, as has been mentioned previously, all you must do is see it in your 'minds eye,' and know that it is coming toward you. Then express the joy, pleasure, and gratitude you will have when you possess it. The object will manifest materially for you as soon as it is possible for it to do so.

I have previously mentioned this above, using the example of calling a twenty-dollar bill to yourself. Once you have mastered that exercise, you might start with other things you wish to have, bearing in mind that you only want one of each of these material objects at this time, unless you desire to have more of the item. Limiting the quantity of items you desire to call to yourself is a necessity; otherwise, you may well find yourself overrun with a large number of similar items.

There is a little story about this; I once badly needed a new typewriter, as several of the metal pieces that struck the ribbon had come off my typewriter. I sent out a call to the universe for one, without setting a limit, and soon I had six typewriters.

19

TECHNIQUES OF
BRAINWASHING AND MIND CONTROL

The following is a list and explanation of the techniques most useful in converting others, changing their minds, or indoctrinating and programming them. Cults, religious organizations, governments, and the military all use these and other techniques, often referred to as Brainwashing, to insure uniformity of thought and action. Indoctrination is used as a more acceptable word describing brainwashing, and conversion is often used as an even more acceptable word describing the change of a person's beliefs from one system to another. However, these are all essentially the same thing, as they are all descriptive of mind control or brainwashing.

1 - Hypnosis

Hypnosis has a very well known reputation as a means of influencing people. Unfortunately, it is not nearly as effective a method of influencing people as its reputation insists it is. Even the strongest and most professionally applied deep post hypnotic suggestion will only last a week, and will often fade away in even less time. Nonetheless, there are several methods of influencing other people that do not seem at first sight to be either hypnotic or anything vaguely like mind control. To the person being influenced they are hypnotic in nature, as these methods prepare the people affected to be open to being influenced by others. We shall concentrate on these methods, as they are the methods most often used by those who wish to influence others, especially when it is desired to influence people in groups or at assemblies.

A - Repetitive Music

Music played as a prelude in churches or many public meetings, is almost expected. The most effective music has hidden messages embedded within it, and is used both as prelude and postludes. For the best results, the same short messages should be played in both instances. The music should have a repetitive beat of between 45 to 72 beats per minute, a beat that urges those who hear it to relax.

{The median frequency of 45 to 72 beats per minute is 58.5 beats. Being just short of one beat per second, it will sound comfortable to most people, as well as relaxing them.}

Repetitive music is one of the most effective ways of preparing people to emotionally accept the following religious service, and most especially accept the words of the sermon spoken by the person leading the service. Music played during the offertory may also be designed to increase donations. A particular rhythm and the sub conscious words, "Give to God," will have this effect.

{A more stimulating beat is usually desired for the offertory, so a beat of about 65 - 70 beats per minute may be used. This is not so stimulating as to break the trance state, but it provides a demarcation indicating that now the person has received, it is time for them to contribute.}

There are several people and firms involved in the process of providing preprogrammed music for churches and other meetings. Using repetitive music to boost attendance and collections is only a secret to those people who have not heard about it.

B – Voice Roll

Professional public speakers, as well as ministers of religion, often use what is known as a voice roll, a paced manner of speaking in rhythm, so there is a delivery of about 45 to 60 words per minute. While it may sound as if the speaker is sounding like a ticking clock, this kind of speech has a subtle hypnotic effect upon those who hear it. Mastering the voice roll is always a worthwhile task for those who wish to become influential in speaking to the public, whether ministers of religion, advocates at law, or in some other business.

Many attorneys, priests, and ministers have taken the opportunity to master this art, knowing it will make the delivery of their words more effective. The voice roll is something Southern Baptist ministers are almost famous for, but they are certainly not the only ones using it.

C – Room "Feel"

The feel, or 'vibration,' of the room a meeting is being held in can have a strong effect on those in the room. Completely aside from any preparation with perfume or incense, using soft fluorescent lighting and regulating the room temperature may be of great assistance in insuring the people in the room are able to enter into the proper semi trance state, or more politely the optimum receptive state, where they are completely open to the words of the speaker addressing them.

{People relax more easily in a warm room, about 72 to 75 degrees Fahrenheit. They are uncomfortable in hot and damp rooms. So the humidity and temperature must both be monitored.}

2 - Peer Group Pressure

Peer pressure, or peer group pressure, is the psychological force applied to an individual or a group, causing the influenced person or group to wish to conform to a social norm presented to them by the group influencing them, a group with which they currently are engaged, or a group to which they belong, or wish to belong.

An example of peer pressure is the desire of a person to be accepted as a member of a social group convincing them to begin smoking, drinking, or taking drugs. This desire for acceptance by the group, and the peer pressure convincing them to do so is the most common reason people begin these self-destructive habits.

People have an emotional need to feel they belong, a desire to connect to others. They want to feel their peers accept them. A variety of pressures to conform are continually being placed on everyone by the society of which they are members. People feel pressure from others concerning the norms of their society, the pressure of the common beliefs of their culture, and most importantly, the pressure of gaining social acceptance from their community, their friends, and their family.

All of these pressures act directly upon everyone, directly influencing their behavior, whether they consider themselves social conformists or rebels. For the most part, *people are not usually consciously aware of the peer pressures placed upon them*. They may only be consciously concerned about the opinion others in their social group may have of them. Those who are conformists wish to be thought of as being just like everyone else. Those who are social rebels, who may believe they have transcended any social pressures, may even believe these pressures have no effect upon them, even though they desire the acceptance of their own socially rebellious group.

Social conformist or rebel, the person is still conforming to the beliefs and behaviors of the group they belong to, and they still seek acceptance of that group. Socially divergent groups of all kinds all have their own rules of procedure, their own beliefs and customs, as well as their own approved and prohibited actions. Those who join any social groups, whether socially conforming or socially divergent, either implicitly or knowingly agree to follow the rules of the group to which they belong. In almost all cases, the person desires to be in the group they belong to, or are presently associated with. Thus the greatest peer pressure they feel, as members of a group, are those extended to them when they are in attendance at any of the group's assemblies or events.

MISCELLANY

Let us examine some of these cultural oddities.

Once a month a group of well-respected community leaders and affluent businessmen gather together in a ritualistic setting. Some of them, previously selected for the purpose, repeat almost the very same words they speak at these assemblies every month. These men, who are perfectly respectable, and usually quite conservative, go through this secret monthly ritualistic experience wearing aprons, and believing their actions are quite normal, if not actually praiseworthy. In their daily working life they would never appear in this way.

These men are freemasons.

In a more divergent setting, there is a group of people living in and around a medium sized city in the eastern United States. These men and women daily dress in, and attend meetings of their organization, wearing clothing of a style last worn in the rural areas of Germany and the Austro Hungarian Empire in the 1850's. Furthermore, they wear this style of clothing every day, all year round, and believe there to be nothing at all unusual about their dress. Their neighbors, who wear more conventional clothing, have grown used to the oddities in dress of these people, and no longer comment on it. Even though their neighbors accept them, many tourists come to this area of the country just to look at these people, as tourists from other areas consider the people to be a curiosity.

These people are old order Amish.

From the above you may understand there are a great many divergent groups, both in dress and behavior. Each of these groups has their own rules and those who are members of the group hold to them in direct proportion to their desire to remain in the group. New members of the group are usually introduced to many of these rules during their process of seeking admission. Those who are born into the group learn these rules as they grow up within the organization.

While a convert to a group may consider their dress or behavior unusual, those who are born into any long established or continuing group consider even the most widely divergent behavior to be perfectly normal. There are thousands of people wearing 'special clothing,' as ordered by their religious beliefs. The old Order Amish are but a minor example of this. Other people (Such as Jews or Mormons) wear special underclothing or odd costumes of all kinds. Still others restrict their diets as ordered by their religion.

Aside from dress and diet, almost all religions, as well as all societies, attempt to regulate the sexual behavior of their members. Any deviation from this prescribed behavior is considered socially divergent, and liable to provoke criticism by the society to which the non-conforming person belongs.

It is in this way societies and religions enforce social conformity upon their members. A survey of history will show social controls, such as male and female circumcision, mating restrictions and other sexual regulations, dietary limitations, and dress or sumptuary regulations, were all introduced to control populations and limit the social and cultural deviation of the regulating society.

The Judas Goat

When a group has culturally divergent views, especially when these views may be shocking to the social beliefs or sensibility of the person seeking admission, peer pressure from the group may be used to bend them into conformity without a word being said. In this case one of the more familiar techniques used is often referred to as the Judas Goat. The Judas Goat is the person whose task is introducing the new member to the practices of the group. They lead the new member into accepting their conformity with otherwise socially divergent practices expected by the group.

If it is desired to convince one or two people of the rightness of the group's beliefs, practices and course in life, a few people who are long standing and believing active members of the group are assigned to the newcomers as guides. Usually there are two people assigned as guides for every person or couple who is to be 'guided.'

MISCELLANY

It is the duty of these guides, who are the Judas Goats, to unconditionally emotionally accept the new members or applicants. Through this unconditional acceptance they guide their charges by their actions, and caution them into understanding the customs, and norms of the group. In this way, through meeting with the people privately and discussing just what is expected of them, the most culturally divergent behavior patterns may be introduced to newcomers without initially shocking, or discouraging them. In this way the new members or applicants soon fit seamlessly into the organization they are joining.

Some examples of this are instances of normally socially divergent nudity in organizations such as Nudist camps, Wiccan, and other similar divergent religious groups, swingers clubs, and similar widely socially divergent groups. In almost all cases there are preliminary introductions, and usually interviews before any widely socially divergent views or beliefs are introduced. The presence of an introductory person or couple introducing the newcomer to the more divergent group eases this transition, by giving the inquirer some indication of what they might expect as members of the group.

The sexual contact and nudity rules of a culture are the two most difficult areas to deal with, as they are the most deeply ingrained into the patterns of the culture. Dress and diet rules are usually easier for new converts to organizations, religious, or otherwise to accept.

In all instances of using a guiding influence, or Judas Goat, in working through peer pressure, the person or people who are guiding the new applicants are deliberately or unknowingly working on the applicant's usually unexpressed desire to 'go along with the crowd.' This desire to be agreeable, and to 'go along with the crowd,' is essentially what peer pressure is.

Peer Pressure, and its effect on people may be illustrated by a story in general circulation in the Middle East:

The Changed Water

There was once a man who for several years had enjoyed a mutually profitable relationship with a powerful Jinni of great strength and ability. On the particular day on which our tale begins, this Jinni came to his human friend and spoke to him in these words:

"Oh associate of mine in both good times and bad, I bear news of grave difficulties to come. It has been ordered by the most high that the waters of the earth shall be changed, to bring upon all men a different condition in their lives. Thus making certain things more difficult for mankind, while giving other things more ease. I have learned this change of water will make it more difficult for you and I to remain in our continual beneficial conversation, and the change may even adversely affect our relationship, as well as our long standing friendship."

"Furthermore, once this change occurs I shall be required to spend at least a year away from you, living in the land of the Jinni, busily occupied with the tasks drawing me there. In recompense, I have prepared this magic glass, which will always contain only the present water common to all humanity. So long as you drink only from it, things in your life shall not change. Thus you can remain an observer to those things which the most high has commanded humanity must now pass through and suffer. Take then this glass, which will always remain full, containing the pure water humanity drinks today, as I must now leave, to go to the land of the Jinn and begin my year of residence there."

"I thank you friend Jinn, and wish you safety and good fortune as you are away from me." The man took the glass and the Jinn disappeared.

At midnight that very night, the highest one changed the waters of all the earth. The next morning the man began drinking the clear water from the glass, as mankind began drinking the changed water. As he drank the pure water, the glass miraculously refilled, just as the Jinn had said, and the man was content.

The man walked out among the people and noticed some of them seemed to be acting oddly, a few of them self destructively. He took neither food nor drink while he was out. Instead, he returned home, made his own meal, and drank only water from the magic glass.

The following day as he walked among the people of his town, he found them to be even more odd in their behavior. Not even those he considered to be friends either spoke to him or addressed him. Once again he took neither food nor drink while he was out, but returned home and drank from the glass.

The third and fourth day after the water changed he did the same. On all of these trips no one had spoken to him, no one had addressed him, and no one seemed even to recognize him. He found this curious, but it made him feel more isolated, more alone, each day. When he returned home from his walk around the town he made and ate his meal and drank water from the glass.

And so it went for several months. No one in his native town spoke to him, no one addressed him by name, and no one even seemed to recognize him. The man was truly alone. He had no conversation, no friends, and no contact with anyone else in his town.

Each day the man would come back to his house and drink from the glass. But finally, after several months being alone, with no conversation, no friends, and no contact with anyone else in his town, he returned to his home in a sour mood. Looking at the glass the Jinni had made for him, he threw it against the wall of his house, destroying it forever.

The man then drank the same water other people used. In a very short time he found he now had conversation with others, he now enjoyed being with his friends, and he resumed his contact with everyone else in his town. He was content, as now he was drinking the changed water, and he was just like everyone else.

Some Examples Of Peer Pressure In Groups

Men fear going to nudist camps because they incorrectly believe they will get an embarrassing erection. Women fear going because they fear their bodies will not match up to the bodies of the other women who may be there, causing them to be hesitant about undressing. Thus some nudist camps have a rule that women need not undress, while men must undress immediately. In theory, this is to discourage those with prurient interests from visiting these camps. In fact, it actually eases the transition in their beliefs.

By following this rule, men learn they will not get an erection, while women discover there are many other women present who present a worse physical appearance then they do. After about a half hour to an hour, the women usually undress. The woman's spontaneous undressing is actually as much from peer pressure as it is from any conscious rational decision on the part of the woman to do so.

A religious cult encouraging group promiscuous sexual encounters among the membership made this a possibility only for those in the highest level of the organization. Combining this with constant pressure on those in the organization to progress from the lowest level to the highest level, made the reward of promiscuous sexual encounters into the carrot, while admonitions to those in the lowest of the three levels to make progress became the stick, or goad driving these newer members forward. The peer pressure was involved in the desire to progress, with the unstated object of accepting sexual promiscuity as a result of this pressure to advance.

3 - Love Bombing

Love Bombing is the process of showing supposedly unconditional love to another person, through friendly conversation, affectionate but non-sexual touching, and full acceptance of the person, by drawing the person into the conversation and activities of the love-bombing group.

The person or people doing the love bombing listen carefully to whatever their victim says, and uses the victims own words, whenever possible, to convince the victim they should join the person or people in whatever their effort is involved in. All through this process they are completely focused on the victim, and are willing to hold hands, hug, or otherwise reassure the victim, providing them with the warm human contact they believe the victim needs.

The goal of love bombing is to convince the victim they have found a supportive group completely and unconditionally accepting them, giving the victim the human warmth and attention they desire. This is accomplished through giving the person focused personal attention and signs of respect, as well as the feeling of their being the recipient of unconditional love.

Attention

Attention is a human requirement, and may be considered to be as necessary and important for maintaining human mental stability as food is to the physical body. Mentally and emotionally required attention may be made available to the victim in an undifferentiated manner. This occurs when those who are 'love bombing,' meet the victim on the street. In the home office or headquarters a trained person may specifically and directly apply this warm unconditional attention to a person. In either case it has the result of making the individual feel accepted, content, and at ease. Naturally, the person enjoys receiving the attention, although they only rarely know just what it is they have received.

One of the oddities about attention is that it is always a one to one transfer. To get attention from someone, you have to pay attention to him or her. Ideally, the transfer of attention is between a man and a woman. This is a non-sexual exchange of attention. The sexual transfer of attention is based on the instinctual drives of the person as a human animal, and is a slightly different thing.

When a group of people is love bombing someone, one person should take the lead in conversing with their target. In almost all cases, this lead person should be a young woman, between nineteen and twenty-five years old. Should there be a negative reaction to the woman initiating conversation with the target, a male of the group in the same age range should be standing by to take over.

A woman should take the lead in love bombing, because most people, both men and women, usually respond well to a woman paying attention to them. Women tend to contract and become defensive when an unknown man begins paying attention to them. Men tend to either become defensive, or more rarely, aggressive when an unknown man begins paying attention to them.

Touching

Touching another person is always a tricky act. In the case of love bombing, the experienced love bomber usually waits until there are signs of submission and obedience coming from the victim before they begin touching them anywhere but briefly on their arms between the elbow and the hand. The first of these signs is usually the victim's agreement with statements made by the person doing the love bombing. If this is followed by smiles and friendly words from the victim, the person leading the love bombing may press forward, including by beginning with a gentle touch on the persons sleeve, between the elbow and the hand.

Once there are a few additional signs of submission and obedience coming from the person, or there is some indication of interest and affection from them, and after a few gentle touches between the elbow and the hand have been made, the love bomber can ask, in an innocent voice, "You look like you could use a hug. Could I give you a hug?" On a positive answer, the woman doing the love bombing should hug the victim. The hug should be brief, three to five seconds, it should be warm, and most importantly, non-sexual.

After the hug has broken, the primary love bomber should be able to place their hand anywhere on the victim's arms without difficulty. If the victim is smiling at this point it is a good clue they are willing for the love bombers to go further. A hand on the upper arm will reinforce this in an affectionate and non-threatening way.

One hug does not a convert make, but if there is any reason to do so, it is a sign the conversation might well be moved to a more agreeable location such as a small coffee shop, a restaurant, or some other location. In the summertime, the conversation may be moved to a park picnic table or bench.

The object of love bombing is always to bring the subject, or victim, into close contact with, or guide them to membership with the group sponsoring the love bombing.

7 - Removal Of Privacy

When you remove privacy from people you are forcing them to begin to conform to your way of belief and thought. Having no privacy, people can no longer privately contemplate things. Being always with others, usually other members of the group, they generally have to adopt the views, beliefs, habits, and customs of the group they are associated with. The closer the group becomes, the more the person becomes uniform in their thoughts, beliefs, and actions. This is the desired standard for any religious group, spiritual, or occult organization, as it makes people as uniform as they can possibly become.

The removal of privacy from people should include the complete elimination of physical privacy as well as the loss of all intellectual privacy. Requiring the person to maintain a daily diary, which is to be reviewed by their mentor or teaching authority once a week, is an example of this.

In some groups, physical privacy is eliminated completely for those in the lower or training ranks of the group administration. This can go so far as to include removing the bathroom and bedroom doors, or requiring group toilet time, showers, and so forth, as well as requiring nudity in the residence areas of the living quarters. These requirements should be enforced on all people in the group.

If there are levels in the elimination of privacy, the total elimination of privacy should be the last level, as it is the most socially divergent. However, this does not mean the partial elimination of privacy cannot have begun earlier. Using open bay barracks helped blend the thoughts of soldiers together when they were introduced to the military in the Napoleonic era. These shared living quarters severely limited privacy, and yet there was little opposition to them. Doing something similar, by putting ten people together living in a large room for example, is a good first step toward the elimination of privacy.

8 - Disinhibition

Disinhibition is the loss of inhibitions through external stimuli such as drugs or alcohol, or in some cases, as a result of brain damage. The word may also be applied in cases where there is unrestrained or riotous behavior, inspired by the loss of inhibitions or a disregard of cultural restraints due to emotional over stimulation. It should be noted this is a loss of the inhibitions due to some known cause, rather than a person not having any restraining inhibitions at all, in which case the person is considered to be uninhibited.

Disinhibited sexual behavior, where the individual does not seem to have any control over their sexual desires seems to be the form of disinhibition most commented on in medical literature. This includes people with gross or immodest conversation, those who inappropriately touch others, and those who publicly commit inappropriate sexual acts, such as public masturbation.

It has also been suggested that disinhibition allows people to commit acts of violence against others, as is found among those committing acts of terrorism. This idea completely ignores that certain religions believe committing acts of violence or terrorism against others, even to the point of killing the innocent, is a meritorious act. These religions even believe committing acts of terrorism meritoriously brings salvation to the one who dies in the attempt to kill others. These religious believers have no inhibition present against committing these violent acts of terror, and some of them even eagerly look forward to doing so.

Disinhibition As Brainwashing

Another form of disinhibition, mentioned as a means of brainwashing, is encouraging child like obedience in the victim by forcing the victim to participate in child like behavior. Treating the victim in a childlike manner, treating the victim as if he were an infant, is one way of forcing the victim to lose their socially imprinted inhibitions, by forcing them to revert to a childlike state in which they are completely dependent upon others. We might observe here that young children are usually allowed no privacy.

Forcing this reverting to a childlike state may include feeding them, speaking to them, and correcting them, using child like expressions and phrasing. The victim should be required to speak in the voice of a child, using childlike words and phrases. The person being infantized must have no responsibility, especially any of the responsibilities granted an adult. Whenever possible, they should be cared for as completely as possible, they should not have any ability to schedule themselves, or care for themselves. Ideally this may be even carried to the point of having the person washed and groomed by a caretaker. This fully disconnects the victims from caring for themselves.

When speaking to the person being infantized, their mentors should always use limited direction and compliments, "You're doing better now." "Try harder and you can do better. I know you can." "You look nice today." "Your hair is much better today." As well as, "Lets take that next step again. We'll just have to practice it until you get it right."

Childish compliments should also be used, "That's cute. It's so sweet to see you do that. You're really very charming when you do it." "Don't you look nice today. I'm so proud of you." "You're really doing very well."

The person this technique is being applied to should be referred to only in terms of the infant or youth. 'New in Christ. Freshly reborn in the Lord. A Babe, or One of the babes. One of the littlest. One of the children of the Lord. A good student. The idea behind this is to limit their authority to the point they surrender themselves completely to the authority and leadership of their attendant or mentor.

This process can be enhanced if the only adult conversation the individual has is 'training,' conducted by an authority in the group on a one to one basis with the person being infantized. This training should include the authority expressing, and the neophyte understanding, the logical need for the individual to release all of their inhibitions, and completely surrender their will to the will of the group. In some cases this can be enhanced by assuring them their surrender to the will of the group is the truest meaning of democracy, or rulership by the people, as in this kind of surrender everyone has a voice and the whole group moves in the direction best suited to all of them.

The rational of infantalizing the victim may be explained by the need for the person to "become reborn," in the group, "Born again in the Lord," and stressing that as a 'child,' in the group the person being infantalized now has to go through the same stages he went through in growing from a baby to adult-hood, releasing himself from all of his former bad education, and learning the new ways of truth and light.

9 - Uncompromising Rules

Any organization should have several firm and fixed rules that cannot be broken without causing the individual to be separated from the group. The imposition of these rules must be absolute, so there should not be a great number of them. When formulating these rules the senior administration must realize they must be held to absolutely.

In a religious organization, these rules are best expressed as non-debatable points of theology. Every organization must carefully think out and establish these points before they begin formulating their organizational matrix, or planning their reli-gious corporation. The difficulty in doing this in a way accept-able to the majority of people shows why most new religions use the Christian matrix, in which the fundamental uncompro-mising rules, rules defining the practice, have already been set in stone. In most Christian groups belief in the Nicean creed is a basic example of an unquestioned rule.

10 - Dress Codes

Dress codes, usually unwritten, are common to all societies. The unwritten social dress code, and any variations from the desired social standard dress, indicates the message being sent by the person deviating from the social standard dress code.

Many religions and social organizations have a dress code they apply to their believers. These dress codes are in addition to, or may even replace, the unwritten social dress code of the society in which they live. The following are examples of a few of these religiously required dress codes:

Old Order Amish wear clothing common in the rural areas of Germany and Austro Hungary in the 1850's. Their women always wear dresses, something almost all religious rules require that women wear. Only Moslem women in America often wear pants, but they wear these pants under the burqas covering them from head to feet.

Jews, especially orthodox Jews, wear skullcaps (Yarmulke) and a religiously prescribed undergarment. Hassidic Jews wear a costume coming from the area of Europe where their particular school (Hassid) of Orthodox Judaism originated. Many of them dress in nineteenth century German formal wear, while others, as those from parts of Poland, dress in an imitation of seventeenth century Polish court costume. Thus it is often possible to identify the particular Hassidic group the man belongs to from their dress.

Roman Catholic and many other Christian religious orders wear a variety of dress known as habits. While most priests wear the "Roman collar," the different habits of the many different Christian religious organizations may often be used to identify to which of these orders of the Christian Religious the individual belongs.

Sikh men wear a turban and other religious garb, including a religious bracelet. Often mistaken for Moslems, they are actually a deviant religion drawn from Hinduism. Sikhs were originally recruited from Hindus of all castes to fight the Moslem invaders of India.

Mormons, members of the LDS church, wear 'Garments,' a set of undergarments worn next to the skin. These garments, worn by both men and women are designed to remind them of the continual presence of God in their lives.

Many of the Hare Krishna's, particularly women in the group, wear Indian Hindu costumes. This usually consists of their wearing saris, and similar more modest garments, following a Hindu pattern of woman's dress.

BRAINWASHING AND MIND CONTROL

There are many other examples of uniforms used in common practice. Many people in public service dress in uniforms. The military, police, and fire fighters are an example of this. Some medical professionals dress in specific garments, nurses wear white clothing, often with caps and pins indicating their school of nursing. Doctors frequently wear surgical scrubs, or they may wear white laboratory jackets over their suit dress of shirt and pants.

In many places around the world students in some schools and universities wear specific dress and costumes, indicating their school affiliation. American Roman Catholic schoolgirls costumes are an example of this.

Identification Of Status Through Dress

In religious and spiritual groups special dress may be used to identify the rank of members of the organization. Examples of this are the colored tabs worn on the 'Roman collars,' of Roman Catholic Priests. Purple tabs indicate Bishops, while red tabs indicate Cardinals.

Inside the more sacred precincts of the organization's buildings, where outsiders are not admitted, special or unusual clothing may be worn. It may be beneficial to have several layers of advancement in this regard, admitting people to higher ranks as they advance within the organization. Thus in the outer or reception area, street dress could be worn, while in the first inner area, more clerical dress could be required except for casual visits from members.

In increasingly more restricted areas of the religious institutions, simple cassocks or shifts may be required, while only special garments might be allowed in the holy of holies. Theological argument may always be provided for any kind of dress the organization seems to believe is suitable.

11 - Chanting Or Singing

Chanting has been used for thousands of years by religious groups, both for getting in touch with their creator, or as a way of meditating. The efficacy of chanting in groups as a means of quieting the mind has been proven over the years by thousands of Buddhist monks all over the world, who chant for hours every day. There are even religious practices which deal entirely with chanting, usually all of them chanting the same mantra every day, whether in groups or alone.

One of the advantages of chanting to the group is that it fills the mind of the chanters with ideas the group wishes to enforce on their members, when they are chanting in an understandable language. If the chanting is in a foreign language, it may be something connecting them sub consciously to the group, rather than manifesting as an idea in the chanters mind.

Chanting is a way of stopping thought, especially chanting in meditation. In time the individual will become far more suggestible, as with habitual chanting they will begin to enter the alpha state at all times, whether they are chanting or not.

I can recall seeing group of Hindu and American students chanting to their teacher as he sat smiling at them on a podium. He told me the more dedicated the students were to him, the greater their chance of spiritual growth. Perhaps this is so, but I really doubt it.

Singing is another means of programming the individual in ways the cult or religion wishes them to accept. Singing in groups, as in a church service, can quite effectively program the individual for life. Robert M Hutchins, the former chancellor of the University of Chicago, once mentioned in an article that he knew he had been raised a protestant, as he would catch himself humming protestant religious songs as he shaved in the morning.

Once these songs and chants become a part of the individuals deep subconscious, the image they project will still come up in the person's mind when any recall of these images is stimulated by something. Often something having no connection at all to the experience of singing or chanting can be a trigger for this involuntary recall. It is because of this that both singing and chanting are of great benefit to the organization encouraging them. They have a strong and permanent programming effect on the individual who chants or sings so enthusiastically.

12 - Confession

Public confession of their faults and past sins is one way of encouraging the destruction of an individual's ego. In this case, both doubt and other concerns must also be addressed in the confession, as the belief is the more the person lets out, the better off they will be as members of the organization. Thus a full and free confession of all past sins and errors is to be encouraged.

In public confession the person confessing does so before his peers, and is usually prompted to go even further by an assistant or a mentor. The goal is to have the individual release his past, and expel all his fears. In addition the person confessing should mention all of his personal weaknesses, as well as express any doubts he may have concerning the organization or its leadership.

Private confession is also to be encouraged, and in some instances the individual may prepare his public confession with the aid of his mentor or teacher. The details of any confession, whether of thoughts or actions, should be recorded and prepared to use against the individual should they later decide to leave the organization. Such confessions have been found to be of great value by some organizations, holding in those who wish to leave, but hesitated because of fear of exposure.

The French Foreign Legion once had their new recruits confess their problems and fears while standing naked and speaking to their fully dressed comrades, who were seated comfortably before them. Supposedly this procedure assisted the new recruits in overcoming their fears.

13 - Financial Commitment

It has been said that where a person's money goes, so goes their heart. Once a person has made a financial commitment to an organization it is usually followed by a desire to participate more fully in the affairs of the organization. A continual financial commitment enhances this effect, and often insures there is a continual involvement in the organization.

In some cases, as when the individual is living in a church or other organization-sponsored facility, they are expected to turn over all of their funds and income to the church. Once this occurs, they have no reasonable out; they have to remain in the organization, as they are unable to go outside it without the funds they have given away. In not a few cases, this may be considered an endowment to purchase their place in the organization or the church. Often the organization receiving the funds has a long and detailed legal contract the donor is required to sign before giving up their wealth to the organization.

14 - Controlled Approval

Controlled, conditional, or limited approval is a means of keeping someone on edge psychologically. Previously examples of this have been mentioned, as saying: "Your hair looks nice today," implying that yesterday it was a mess. Every compliment given anyone, and there should be lots of them, will be phrased in such a manner as to express limited approval of the person, their work, or their actions. Doing this takes practice, so the person making compliments must first master the art of making compliments expressing limited approval, and giving tightly controlled approval to others.

15 - No Questions

In most organizations there are those questions, which are not ever to be asked. They always deal with things that are just not to be questioned by anyone in the organization. In more autocratic organizations there are no questions allowed about anything having to do with the administration and leadership of the organization.

Although it may not always seem like it, the more vibrant and growing organizations have fewer questions that are not to be asked. In these organizations absolutely everything is up for argument or discussion. Early Christianity was like that, as each of the churches had their own theology. There were battles fought, to say nothing of arguments, over such subjects as the divinity of Christ, the nature, and manner of his death, whether or not he resurrected in the spirit or in the body, and whether he was the exclusive Son of God or if that was a condition shared by all mankind. Most such questions would not be allowed to be asked today.

20

WRITING AFFIRMATIONS AND SCRIPTS
TO INFLUENCE YOURSELF OR OTHERS

All scripts and affirmation should be written as positive statements of fact. For example. "Your body is healing itself," rather than; "Your body will heal itself."

The reason for this is that with any mention of time the sub conscious believes it does not have to do anything; it can just wait whatever out. Since the real purpose of affirmations and scripts is to convince the sub conscious mind to act, this is a self-defeating way to go about it.

When you tell the sub concious mind something as a fact, it will accept what you tell it as a fact. If it has to do something to make that fact occur, it will (In most cases) do whatever is necessary. If you tell it something will happen in time, it will patiently wait for whatever is to happen, whether it ever happens or not.

About the worst things to say is, "You will get better." The sub conscious sees this as a platitude, and will do nothing to make it happen. You must avoid using platitudes and similar stroking statements, they have no effect on the sub conscious.

WRITING AFFIRMATIONS AND SCRIPTS

The well-known affirmation;

>Every day in every way
>I am getting better and better.

Often works because it is put in a positive statement and the time limitation within it is set to "every day." In this case the sub concious mind looks for some improvement every day, and whether the individual is consciously aware of it or not, the sub conscious might just deliver something that is useful to them.

Affirmations to heal illnesses, when used in remote influence are often placed in the following form. "You have something within you which is not beneficial to your being. It is now necessary that you remove this from your being. Over the next few weeks you will completely eliminate this negative influence from within your being. At the end of this time, you will be restored to full and vibrant health."

I have used this affirmation in remote influence many times, occasionally with remarkable success. In many cases this can produce a remission or cure of a physical illness. When doing this affirmation it is of value to visualize the individual as they were when in a healthy and happy state.

Breaking bad habits can be accomplished by telling the person they are someone who does not like to do what they have been doing. As and example, "You have learned you are someone who does not like smoking. You find that smoking, and the smell of cigarettes disgusts you." Telling the person to stop smoking is not necessary at this point. Once they make that decision consciously, you can help them out by telling them. "You do not suffer from the pangs of withdrawal that some people have (or feel) when they stop smoking."

Affirmations and prayers are usually done by the people themselves, although others can do them, by saying they make the prayer or do the affirmation, "In the name of," the person they are being done for. This may be a much weaker method or it may work as well as the person doing the affirmations themselves, there is no telling just how it will come out. However, if the person is unable to do the affirmation or prayer themselves it is certainly worth trying.

MISCELLANY

Scripts for remote influence are very similar to affirmations, but many times they are given to people without the person having any prior understanding of the work being done, or any desire to make the changes being suggested to them. Seduction scripts are usually of this kind, and if they are gradually increased in intensity, they are often very successful. Those that fail are usually those scripts that progress too rapidly. This is also true of healing scripts, as the introduction, that there is a difficulty present is important. The sub conscious mind may not recognize even the most severe condition as being harmful.

It should be obvious that shorter affirmations and scripts are more likely to be successful than longer affirmations and scripts. However, I have seen scripts that are two or three typewritten pages long. Some times these longer scripts are successful, in other instances they are not. Here the difference seems to be how deeply the person giving the script can penetrate into the sub conscious mind of the person they are working with. In general, shorter scripts are more successful, and more easily retained in the mind of those being influenced.

MISCELLANY

40,715

Made in the USA
San Bernardino, CA
25 May 2015